20th CENTURY ARCHITECTURE:

A READER'S GUIDE

Berthold Lubetkin and Margaret Church in a speedboat belonging to
Ove Arup. The figure in the background is Fred Lassere. The
photograph was taken by Peter Moro in 1937 or 1938. Source:
Courtesy Sasha Lubetkin.

20th **CENTURY ARCHITECTURE:**
A READER'S GUIDE

Martin Pawley

Architectural Press

OXFORD   AUCKLAND   BOSTON   JOHANNESBURG   MELBOURNE   NEW DELHI

Architectural Press
An imprint of Butterworth-Heinemann
Linacre House, Jordan Hill, Oxford OX2 8DP
225 Wildwood Avenue, Woburn, MA 01801-2041
A division of Reed Educational and Professional Publishing Ltd

   A member of the Reed Elsevier plc group

First published 2000

© Martin Pawley 2000

British Library Cataloguing in Publication Data
Pawley, Martin
   20th century architecture: a reader's guide
   1. Architecture, Modern – 20th century
   I. Title II. Twentieth century architecture
   724.6

ISBN 0 7506 4635 7

Library of Congress Cataloguing in Publication Data
A catalogue record for this book is available from the Library of
Congress

Composition Scribe Design, Gillingham, Kent
Printed and bound in Great Britain by Biddles Ltd, www.Biddles.co.uk

Contents

Preface

Any attempt to compile a general purpose reader's guide to the architectural writing of the 20th century using recently published books for ease of access is bound to be questionable. First, and most fundamentally, the selection of works will not evenly cover the whole century but instead be crowded into the last third of it. This will inevitably mean that later books – even if some of the most important of them are later editions of earlier books – will be employed as a means of accessing earlier periods, rather than being treated as ends in themselves. This in turn will make the reviews discursive and thematic, rather than narrowly focused on the opinions expressed by the book's authors. In short, while the books cited in the bibliography may offer a fair spread across the century, the books reviewed must focus on the key historical episodes and controversies, and dwell on the personalities who played the most prominent parts in them. Thus while there may perhaps seem to be too much about Frank Lloyd Wright, Le Corbusier, Mies van der Rohe, Berthold Lubetkin, Richard (now Lord) Rogers, Leon Krier, Charles Jencks and Prince Charles, there is nothing at all about Oscar Niemeyer or Sir Norman Foster, two of the greatest architects of the century. This is because the first is a man whose dramatic struggles took place far away from the Anglo-Saxon world and the second is a genius at avoiding embroilment in controversy yet paying no price in compromise.

Second to the use of books and reputations as building blocks rather than as individual creative works must come the randomness and sheer subjectivity of the choice of titles made – which will therefore satisfy few persons apart from the author. Many of the works chosen for review, the author freely concedes, are not of great value, although the importance ascribed to the subjects they address may even the balance somewhat. Nonetheless it would be fair to regard most of them as second rate contributions to fields better attacked or defended by others who came before them.

As a subset of this admission of subjectivity and chance must come the Western World origin of practically all the books selected. This, in an age of instantaneous global communications and worldwide architectural practice, is tantamount to parochialism – unless of course one accepts that the vast majority of the architecture produced and discussed during the 20th century was indeed national, even though the majority of the architecture of the 21st may not be.

The third aspect of this book requiring a prefatory comment is the way in which, in its pages, almost the whole spread of the century past emerges as an era dominated by vicissitudes of the Modern Movement: that explosive phenomenon in the history of architecture whose effects seem inexhaustible and whose influence will clearly stay with us for decades, if not centuries to come.

In this compilation I have elected to confront all these problems head-on. The first charge of abusing chronology by making later books serve for earlier periods is frankly accepted, indeed invited: the books listed here represent my own choice and opportunity reading during 35 years of studying, practicing, teaching and criticizing architecture. The review section, covering 80 volumes, and making up the bulk of the book's contents, comprises a selection from the large number of books that I begged to or agreed to review for newspapers and architectural magazines between 1967 and 1999. A modest advantage of this short time frame is that most are easily available.

As for the problem of Anglo-centric bias, this too has deep foundations. Because the collection of reviews assembled here is in no sense an academic study, it is better to view it as a personal attempt to relate judgements made in the course of a career to the unique perspective offered by the end of a century. Inevitably, nearly all the architects whose work is dealt with here are English, continental European or North American. In this sense the Anglo-Saxon world, with its seemingly inextinguishable reverence for the *idea* of architecture (coupled, it must be said, with a breathtakingly fickle capacity to dismiss the reality of it as soon as its novelty has waned), is being made to do a job that a wider sweep might have transformed into something rather different and altogether more imposing. But then again it is the particularities of all cultures that make up their history and provide the signposts we recognize when we explore them, not the generalities.

The final problem area, that of the total dominance of the Modern Movement, must surely be less debatable. Modernism, the magnificent mutiny against historicism, revivalism and the vernacular that presented our century with the prospect of a culture of buildings as instruments, instead of monuments (as the Czechoslovak painter Karel Teige memorably defined it in 1933), does indeed bestride the 20th century like a colossus. In all its decades, from its first stirrings in the Edwardian age to its depoliticized return at the very end of the century as evidence of 'up to dateness', its presence has been central to the fortunes of architecture, whether as an avant garde tendency, a rising star, a revolutionary challenge, a global orthodoxy, an unmitigated evil, a fallen giant or (perhaps) as a resurgent force that is even now gathering strength.

Introduction

For hundreds of years before the first stirrings of the Modern Movement, knowledge was considered to be a matter of the printed word. Everything from architecture to zoology was catalogued and remembered by means of books. Storing knowledge was therefore considered solely as a matter of storing books and this restriction has never been questioned by architectural writers. Over the course of the 20th century, however, it has become increasingly evident that the shape of knowledge is changing. In the McLuhan age, while they may still be proliferating in numbers, books have lost their privileged status. Modern information systems have revealed them for what they are, clumsy, limited capacity curiosities, like old gramophone records.

As a result even the rarest and most valuable books can no longer transcend their origins as compressed rags, sewn together with cotton thread. Almost unbelievably, in our world of industrial design, composites and miniaturization, their covers are made from the skins of animals and their titles are crudely embossed by hand. Even their type was set, letter by letter, in wooden frames. Such books have ceased to be classed as knowledge, they have become antiques, sought only by collectors.

Today we access knowledge by different means. We absorb it from moving pictures, live and recorded sound, signals bounced off satellites, documents duplicated, faxed, e-mailed or displayed on monitors in airports and railway stations, or else we seek it out on the Internet. At the end of the 20th century even the newest books have become little more than the 'cassettes' of an old-fashioned signalling system, containers of a knowledge that must be scanned and digitized in order to be made truly available as information. Other systems work better. Even as our knowledge sources proliferate we miniaturize their output, recording it invisibly on magnetic tapes, microchips, disks, CDs and crystals of enormous capacity.

Ever since the 20th century began, the world of knowledge has been living through a volcanic eruption of new technologies whose effect has been, if not to render the book entirely obsolete, at least to make its place in the future doubtful. Certainly from 15th century to the present the overwhelming bulk of the world's knowledge has been contained in books. But no such certainty exists about the future. We have discovered that, just as a refrigerator is no more than a volume of cold air, so is a book no more than a quantity of information. In this respect architectural books, heavily dependent on imagery as most of them are, have now become hostages to fortune in ways unimaginable to most of those who wrote and read them in the years 1900–1999. This is a factor to be borne in mind when considering the collection of books reviewed here. All of them without question already belong to an historical period that is not the same as our own.

As one or two architectural historians might agree, the shadow of Modernism fell heavily over the first three-quarters of the 20th century, during which time the literature of architecture, good and bad, was clearly divided between traditionalist/revivalist and Modernist/progressive schools of thought. During that time the struggle between these two ideologies was given added force by their role in four key historical events. In chronological order these were: the destruction of the old Empires of Europe and creation of new republics in the aftermath of the Great War of 1914–1918; the suppression of Modern architecture in Germany and the Soviet Union during the 1930s; the overthrow of the forces of Fascism at the end of World War Two and the consequent triumph of Modernism; and the shock administered to the economies of the Western world by the oil price increases of 1973–1979 which for the first time related environmental concerns to the process of designing buildings. The literature of the final quarter of the century, from 1975 until the present, has continued to pay lip service to this last factor, but not to the exclusion of the struggle between the two principal architectural ideologies, which has entered a new phase, emulating the new relationship of the two super powers of the Cold War, by fusing into an uneasy synthesis. In this respect the last quartile of the century has seen the emergence of a new scale of operations, and new goals and constraints in architecture that require to be described in a different way.

In my choice of books I have endeavoured to allow Modernism its great preponderance, without neglecting the opposing views that were most forcefully presented during two great periods of attack; the first delivered by the neo-Classical totalitarian European regimes of the 1930s and the second by the Royalist classical revival movement of the 1980s.

In the last year of the 20th century it seems that the echoes of both these great conflicts have died down and, as a result, the literature of the present is by comparison superficial and inconsequential. This, however, may be an illusion. Like the writings of philosophers, books of architecture can be volatile in their ascribed importance. Some believe that even now the afterglow of the Modern versus Traditional controversies of the past is enough to bring about a re-ignition of these old hostilities at any time. Others see an entropic decline in the force of architectural writing, a phenomenon that follows the waning of historical consciousness, the progressive consumerization of architectural ideas, and, perhaps most of all, the vast inroads made by colour photography into the appearance and meaning of books.

While architectural writers will always strive to accord their subject at least a vestige of transcendental significance, it is true that, with the arrival of the era of colour photography and sponsored publishing, what they write has literally dwindled in size, so that it is often perceived as no more than a restful grey patterning, a Berber carpet between large pieces of furniture. In the same way, plans and sections, once considered essential to the understanding of the design of buildings, are now either uninformatively bare, confusingly overprinted on pictures or text or tint, or withheld entirely, allegedly in the interests of security.

However, the consumerization of graphic design in architecture has not been without its benefits. If the literature of architecture at the close of our century does seem to be overshadowed by four-colour reproduction and deserted by first-rate minds, its reputation amongst ordinary people has not yet suffered. In the public mind the mysteries of architecture, and the grandiloquent irresponsibilities of architects, remain limitless. Never mind that today's thin, large-format architectural picture books more and more resemble fat fashion magazines, the two have much in common.

ARCHITECTURE AND FASHION

Neither architecture nor fashion is routinely renewed by fresh thought and new discoveries: for the most part both survive by plagiarism and repetition. Indeed they rapidly lose their bearings when deprived of a steady diet of precedent and example. Because of this similarity, writing about fashion illuminates the nature of writing about architecture. Typically, in neither field does repetition prevent writers from finding things 'shocking' or detecting in them a 'New Look' (which is really an old look subject to its latest re-release). Both fields too are alike in their capacity to arouse from time to time a fickle, unpredictable, occasionally passionate and always ill-informed public interest. Their means of stimulating this interest is unchanging: it is invariably achieved by exaggeration and oversimplification, and examples of it fall readily to hand. When the fashion historian Aileen Ribiero generalizes wildly in *Fashion and Morality* (London 1986) that 'The best dressers of every age have always been the worst men and women'; her statement, in its glib and sweeping unprovability, is a perfect example. One thinks immediately of Richard Buckminster Fuller's claim that 'The answer to the housing problem lies on the way to the Moon', Jean Nouvel insisting 'I would not only die for architecture, I would kill for it', Sir Norman Foster alerting us to the fact that, 'I can glance at my watch and know exactly what the time is, just by the position of the hands' (in a 1995 advertisement for Rolex watches) or indeed any of the impossible axioms of the great Modern pioneer Le Corbusier, such as 'In architecture there is no such thing as detail, everything is important'. Lack of caution, alongside ignorance, is endemic in both fields. At the heart of it lies an unmistakable streak of amateurism, an important and generally well-hidden trait that gives much away. Architecture, like fashion, is a business with a large amateur following possessing an exaggerated idea of its importance in the world.

There is another interesting reflection on the nature of architectural writing to be drawn from the comparison of fashion and architecture. Notwithstanding its far greater cost and unconscionable gestation time compared to any creation of the fashion industry, architecture that is exhaustively written about, like collections that are extravagantly admired, tends to be functionally insignificant and well out of the economic mainstream. The house built in 1948 by Charles and Ray Eames out of ordinary manufacturer's catalogue components has been endlessly enthused over since its completion, but in itself it is modest and unassuming, barely a dwelling at all in that it has hardly ever been lived in. Mies van der Rohe's Farnsworth House of 1949 may represent the other extreme of industrial elegance, but it too is barely a dwelling, more a white-painted steel and glass sculpture in an out of the way place. A house with nowhere to hang pictures except the bathrooms – whose doors must therefore be kept open to preserve them. These impractical masterpieces exactly parallel the exclusive collections of haute couture: much illustrated, much commented on, but seldom actually worn by anybody.

In architecture obscurity, demolition, out of the way-ness and modesty are no barriers to fame. In the same way as fashion designers might like to use obscure Mongolian yarns, laboratory synthetic fabrics or unusual dyeing procedures, architectural historians and critics, eager to build up their own stable of talent, like to bet on young outsiders or assiduous networkers. In this sense there is no excess of fashion writing that architecture cannot match. Canonical buildings, the building blocks of critical theory have often not even been seen by those who write about them, discuss them or use them as stepping stones to prove an argument. The most often cited example is the German pavilion built at the International Exposition held in Barcelona in 1929. Designed by Mies van der Rohe, this structure was not merely temporary and purposeless in an economic and political sense, but can only have been seen by a tiny minority of the writers who subsequently extolled its magnificence. The secret ingredient of course was the ceaseless publication of photographs of it. The famous Herbert Matter photographs of this small building, taken before the exhibition opened, were subsequently purchased by the New York Museum of Modern Art and have endlessly been replicated ever since. They ensure the proliferation of its pristine image for the rest of recorded time. Even today, when a replica of the pavilion exists on its original site, the monochrome photographs of the original are often preferred by picture editors.

Throughout the 20th century completed buildings judged to be culturally significant have been presented to a limited number of people – roughly evenly made up of potential patrons, potential critics and photographers – in a manner reminiscent of the final dress rehearsal of a play. The writing that results from such *vernissages* has been no better, and certainly no more illuminating, than the writing that results from exclusive fashion shows. Shrill, partisan and for the most part unreadable after the passage of a week or two – when it begins to repeat itself – it rapidly dissolves into a blur of endless applause for everything. Nonetheless it makes up the bulk of the sum total of writing devoted to architecture at the end of the 20th century, just as it made up the bulk of the writing devoted to architecture at the close of the 19th century. Then, as now, the authentic literature of architecture, the literature written by architects about new ideas and technologies, and the literature written about architects dealing with the political and social responsibilities they invoke, constitutes an infinitesimal part of the total. It may have been by definition, the purest and most effective part, but as our century has advanced towards its conclusion, it has been crowded out by an indiscriminate flood of pictures and praise behind which other forces have gathered strength.

THE IMPERIAL AGE 1900–1918

The Imperial Age was a period dominated by the issues of the 19th century and should properly be regarded as a continuation of it. To this day this period remains the last to have been in thrall to the indisputable authority of historical example, which was taken to be the basis for all architectural theory. During the Imperial Age the issues confronted by architectural writers were overwhelmingly aesthetic, and concerned with materials and technology only in a style-dominated sense. Nor were the writers themselves driven by radical social or political ideas, except in so far as these emanated from the ideas of craft-socialism and a dogged resistance to the unstoppable progress of industrialization. The most admired English language theorists on the brink of the 20th century were Augustus Welby Pugin (1812–1852), William Morris (1834–1896) and John Ruskin (1819–1900), none of whom seriously addressed such issues as productivity, cost, adaptability, thermal performance or communications in terms that would be understood today. In England, only towards the end of the 19th century did their emphasis upon notions of truth, honesty and craftsmanship begin to give place to a macroscopic level of thinking more appropriate to the ideologically mobilized political forces of the time. In Imperial terms this new thinking expressed itself in ambitious urban projects, like London's 'Imperial Processional Way' which was proposed to stretch from Buckingham Palace to the Guildhall via two new Thames bridges and a vast 'Imperial Parliament' on the South Bank. These grandiloquent projects are described in Thomas Metcalf's *An Imperial Vision* (London 1989) and make a worthy comparison with the nascent Modern notions inspired by revolutionary events and Utopian writings originating on the

European mainland. Their echo in England was relatively muted, but among the leading figures responding to these new ideas were writers of world influence. Pioneers of the proto-Modernist view were Ebenezer Howard (1850–1928), whose seminal volume *Tomorrow: A Peaceful Path to Real Reform* (London 1898) launched the garden city movement, and, in architecture itself, William Lethaby (1857–1931), whose *Architecture, Mysticism and Myth* (London 1892) is worthy of note, though less strident than the polemical essays of Adolf Loos (1870–1933), which were originally published in Vienna in the late 1890s and only later translated.

Nothing changed with the advent of the new century. Most mainstream architectural writing in the 14 years before the outbreak of the Great War continued to lean heavily on the academic historicism of the past. In this mainstream, non-political aesthetic movements like Art Nouveau and the Vienna Secession joined the dominant Greek, Roman and Gothic Revival styles, and became subsumed into an exotic Edwardian style expressive of the grandeur and triumphalism of the age of colonial Empires. As in the decade preceding the turn of the 19th century, proto-Modern writings continued to appear, but the importance they are accorded today is anachronistic. In fact it is not widely understood, even today, that Pioneer Modern polemicists like the Italians Sant' Elia and Chiattone, like the authors of the *Futurist Manifesto* of 1914, now enjoy an importance that is entirely the creation of art historical research. In the mainstream world of European architecture in the years to 1914 their significance was negligible. If there was a broad based idea of progress, it was focused not on the Modernist avant garde, but on the commercial architecture of the US, where spectacular high-rise buildings and large-scale industrial structures were already being assembled, or upon Wilhelmine Germany, where the organized development of industrial design was far ahead of other countries.

Because of the sheltered dissonance of its own literature, it is only in retrospect that we can see how the distinctive architecture of the last decades of the Imperial Age was in fact 'ghosted' by engineers and made possible by the miracle materials of 19th century engineering, such as steel, concrete and plate glass. The first recognition of this 'deception' did not arise until the post-Great War period which enjoyed a powerful revulsion against many of the beliefs and methods of its predecessor. A good example of this proto-Modern charge of 'deception' is to be found in the view of the pre-1914 period taken by the critic John Betjeman when he wrote disparagingly in *Ghastly Good Taste* (London 1933) of a pre-war 'system which allowed "gentlemen" to show off their knowledge of period, while the all-important engineers had their good work hidden'.

In a manner that is even more visible today than it was when Betjeman wrote, we can see that not just an era but a whole process of continuity in architecture died with the coming of the Great War in Europe. The accusation that Imperial architecture was merely decorated engineering is only a small part of it, no more than a mirror image of the Classical Revivalist's later claim that Modern Architecture was no more than engineering stripped of its architectural dress. To find distinctions where there are no differences is of course the art of the polemicist in any field, and it is true that a kind of stripped classicism, termed 'neo-Georgian' in England, did survive the war and continued to conceal its crucial engineering underpinnings as before, but the real blow to tradition in architecture was something fundamental to the whole process of construction. In the course of the war the myriad crafts incorporated into building over the preceding century, as well as the exact relationships of rank, order and responsibility that had governed the operations of the construction industry for centuries, were swept away. The magnitude of the change was so vast that it took a later generation of observers, e.g. Niels Prak, in *Architects: The Noted and the Ignored* (New York 1984), to see how one era of construction did end, and another begin, somewhere in the 4 years of deadly trench warfare that impoverished Europe.

THE MODERN AGES 1919–1973

The second ideological era of the 20th century, and creatively the most important, was the Modern period. This was an epoch

ushered in by the Great War of 1914–1918. With the passage
of time it has become increasingly difficult for writers to understand the scale of the disaster faced by the forces of tradition
after this massive conflict. In addition to a death toll of more
than 35 million, this industrialized struggle swept away the
accumulated territories, social and administrative systems, cultural and social assumptions of three great empires – Imperial
Germany, Imperial Austria-Hungary and Imperial Russia. With
them went a continuity in architectural thought that successive
generations of conservative theorists and practitioners have
striven to recreate ever since, with limited success. So fundamental was this break with the past that it can be likened to a
mutiny. A reversal of the chain of command that began with the
repudiation of the art historical value system – which was seen
as part and parcel of the inflexible Imperial social order that
had led to the war – and ended with the collapse of a new form
of social patronage, driven by governments, mass political
movements and programmes for social betterment, some 50
years later. The great ideological documents of Modernism
belong to this period, as do the best popularizing Modernist
texts and also the most savage denunciations from the histori-
cist camp, thrown onto the defensive for the first time.

Compared to, say, the advent of Greek Revival architecture –
whether in its Regency or Edwardian manifestation – the arrival
of Modern Architecture represented a vast upheaval. It was a
revolutionary change rather than a minor aesthetic event. Just
as it took the Great Fire of London in 1666 to put an end to
timber construction in the city and give birth to brick, so was
the destruction of the two interconnected World Wars necessary to establish a new architecture. The interaction of the two
wars (recovery from one and preparation for the next, followed
by recovery from the second), created a vast trauma of some
40–50 years. This period was characterized by radical changes
in the 'genetic frequency' of several building types, which in
turn were the cause of changes in the 'genetic frequency' of certain approaches to design. Just as a natural cataclysm like an ice
age can change a species population in both affected and unaf-
fected areas by means of migration, so did the great upheaval of
the wars change the meaning of architecture.

During the course of the wars themselves many hundreds of thousands of buildings were destroyed; maintenance and new construction ceased, and material and manpower shortages persisted until long after each of the conflicts was over. In Europe and Asia the direct effect of these wars upon the built environment lasted for at least half a century, in some ways it still persists. As a direct consequence of bombing, land warfare and neglect, massive post-war building programmes were undertaken in housing, schools, hospitals and factories. During this period of accelerated construction revolutionary new designs, building materials and techniques which minimized material and manpower input gained within a few years a prominence that they would not otherwise have attained in a century. The old craft-enthralled 'shape' of architecture was bent to social and political ends, and its practitioners (and their apologists) were made to make the desperate culturally acceptable. And they did so.

This was truly an era of crisis. The tradition of all that went before was jettisoned. Knowledge of traditional materials and methods could not coexist with the creation of new ones. In an unprecedented rupture, the wisdom of the old building trades was cast aside and the profession of architecture began to re-educate itself from the scientific laboratory.

During the 20 years' peace between the wars there was virtually no criticism of architecture in the sense of regular appraisals of new buildings as they were put up. Architecture had come to be regarded as a professional mystery, and so much emphasis was put on new planning and building techniques and new aesthetic allegiances that only those within the Modern Movement, only architects in fact, were thought to be qualified to act as critics. They in turn were reluctant to criticize their fellow practitioners.

In the same way the ideological stance of the profession's leaders encouraged the statement and restatement of principles rather than the construction of examples, which were in fact few and far between at the time. The critics of the period were concerned with polemical arguments about Modernism. They were dedicated to a cause and not only did they regard the kind of building that did not adhere to the cause to be

unworthy of serious criticism, they also could not allow the
buildings that did adhere to the cause to be criticized for fear
of weakening or betraying it.

This ideological paralysis exactly identifies the difference
between criticism of performance and criticism of intention that
has been central to the literature of architecture in the 20th century. Dogmatic, prejudiced and fiery the period between the
wars was a period of ideological struggle, but it also saw the
appearance of the best and most influential architectural writing of the last 100 years. Writing that reflected the spirit of an
era of innovation presaged by what we might term the 'isolated
genetic experiments' of the Imperial Age. By 1945 these 'experiments' had so far proved themselves to the politicians as to
share the status of 'Modern Medicine' or even 'Modern
Science'. In the crucial post-World War Two decade 'Modern
Architecture' was accepted in the utilitarian spirit of rationing,
popular mobilization, mass production and planning.

During the post-war years many thousands of architects
were trained as rapidly as possible and sent out to practice
their art. In Britain the number of architects in practice rose
rapidly, from 6000 to 20 000 in the 20 years from 1945.
Planning called for huge public housing programmes, the construction of 200 New Towns, the removal of industry to parts
of the country with high unemployment, and the construction
of a 2000 mile motorway network to link everywhere to
everywhere else. All this work was begun, but much of it was
ill-synchronized and poorly executed. For decades public sector borrowing cushioned overmanning, poor management
and obsolescence in everything from education to ship building. It was upon this scene that the energy crisis and the great
inflation of the 1970s descended.

THE POST-MODERN AGE 1974–2000

When, on October 6th 1973, engineering units of the
Egyptian army crossed the Suez Canal and invaded the Sinai
desert, they began the post-Modern age. By an elaborate train

of events their action, which led to the quintupling of the price of Arab oil and the spectre of fuel starvation in the US, in turn created an economic crisis which overturned the high-energy economies of the Western World and slowly but surely began to close down the high levels of government spending on social architecture that had been maintained for nearly 30 years. Robbed of its public sector sources of finance, within a decade of 1973 Modern Architecture was defenceless and faced with eclipse.

Despite emerging from the Second World War as an unchallenged symbol of planning, social welfare and democracy, with a mandate to rebuild devastated cities everywhere, Modern Architecture could not survive without the funding generated by its socialistic ideological underpinnings. When Western governments abandoned deficit spending and turned their backs on welfare spending, welfare architecture proved surprisingly vulnerable. In due course its fall was to usher in the third and final phase of 20th century architecture in the shape of the post-Modern age.

The first and most important escape route from the wrecked ship of Modernism was to learn to bow to the simple notion of the superiority of the past. This idea was succinctly encapsulated in a leader in *The Times* published in 1981: 'The thing a building most needs to secure public affection is to have been standing a very long time. This is a quality hard to achieve in new construction'. Hard, yes, but not impossible. By the mid-1980s the new Heritage culture had consolidated its power throughout the land. Its watchdog voluntary societies were organized into a seamless network represented at the highest levels of government by a publicly funded umbrella organization called English Heritage. Twenty thousand architects, many of them trained in the 1960s when they were told that their task was to design 'a new, organized surface of the earth', put away their plans and put up no resistance. Taken together the conservation organizations disposed of hundreds of millions of pounds in commissions for restoration and repair. Besides, there was a new generation of architects coming to maturity prepared to design according to the discipline of Classical architecture as though the Industrial

Revolution and the Modern Movement had never happened.

If an initially passive, but soon active collaboration with the regime of the conservationists was the first future to beckon from beyond Modern Architecture, the second involved the development of a new post-Modern style of design. This tendency, which rapidly became a 'movement', was not the outcome of architectural practice. Instead it came to life in the studies and lecture rooms of schools of architecture where today's architectural thinkers are obliged to invent movements to advance careers which – no less than those of miners and fishermen – depend on productivity.

The starting date for post-Modernism in architecture is characteristically obscure. Some believe it is clearly foreshadowed in the Classical caryatids supporting the entrance canopy designed by Berthold Lubetkin (1900–1991) for his otherwise ruthlessly modern 1938 'Highpoint II' flats in North London, but leading architectural historians do not share this view. Nikolaus Pevsner, writing in 1966, claimed that Sir Denys Lasdun's Royal College of Physicians building in Regent's Park was the first post-Modern building. Charles Jencks, the style's most loquacious analyst, claimed in 1977 that post-Modernism began where Modernism ended – in his view with the commencement of the demolition of a notorious Saint Louis high rise housing project – Pruitt Igoe – 'on July 15th 1972 at 3.32 p.m.'.

This variety of dates is characteristic, in some ways it resembles the residual doubts about authenticity that haunt so many of the world's great paintings. In any case the prospects for post-Modernism in architecture have been settled more readily than its origins. Some post-Modernists proved adept at attracting popular support and patronage and moving through to immense commissions; notably James Stirling (1923–1992), Michael Graves (*b.* 1934) and Terry Farrell (*b.* 1941), but others seem to be unable to satisfy the more discriminating and powerful leaders of the conservation and Classical Revival lobby. For these persons the built environment as a museum of Georgian buildings interlaced with high tech science parks is a saleable commodity, where collections of post-Modern architectural jokes are not. The non-specific historicism of post-Modern design may go down well enough where even the most erudite critic sees no objection to Corinthian capitals and cyclopean masonry side by side in the same structure – or 'more Venetian windows than there are in the whole of Vicenza' – as Philip Johnson (*b*. 1910) proudly boasted of his enormous International Place complex in Boston. But in the end the greatest enemy of the post-Modern in architecture is not the future but the past. In building, as in TV dramatizations, a heritage audience is inclined in the long run to prefer straight copies of the classics.

Classical Revival and post-Modernism were two architectural escape routes from Modernism: the third was 'High-Tech'. The term itself was originally a mid-1970s American descriptor for a style of interior decoration based on the use of wall-painted supergraphics, alloy car wheels as tables, industrial lighting and storage fittings, and other non-domestic items. From there it leaped across the Atlantic to describe the kind of structurally expressive lightweight architecture that had succeeded the heavy steel frame style introduced by Mies van der Rohe. This architecture, exemplified in Britain by the CLASP prefabricated school system, had originally been called 'Modern' too but, in the wake of an increasing use of light, high-strength alloy and composite components, the new term seemed appropriate. Furthermore, the new name was not burdened with overtones of the Modern failure.

Once again it is difficult to date the transition from modern to 'High-tech' architecture. A glance at the superstructure of any 20th century warship is reminiscent of the clip-on modules of an oil platform and thus of, say, the roof of the Inmos building designed by Richard Rogers (*b*. 1935), if not the service towers of the Lloyd's building itself. In the same way the design of the superstructure of warships, like the bridge of the cruiser HMS *Belfast* (1938), with its bare finishes and exposed servicing, clearly resembles many current 'High-tech' buildings. But the earliest architectural contender is probably Gunnar Asplund (1904–1945), with his lightweight structures for the 1930 Stockholm exhibition, temporary buildings, like the mast-supported structures designed by George Fred Keck in the years before World War Two.

Generally characterized as the acceptable face of Modernism, 'High-Tech' architecture occupies a unique status. In Britain it is indissolubly associated with the work of Sir Norman Foster (*b*. 1935), Sir Richard Rogers, Nicholas Grimshaw (*b*. 1941) and other younger practitioners. In the 1980s the global success of these designers led to 'High-Tech' architecture being dubbed in some quarters 'The English style'.

Taking all these elements into account, it is probably true to say that the post-Modern age, the age of the present, is marked by a pluralism, not of consent, as in the years before 1914, nor of conflict, as in the inter-war years of 1919–1939, but of nihilistic theorylessness. As its name somewhat implies, our post-Modern age is an age without ideology, an age in which all previous tendencies uneasily coexist without conviction and without power.

Only in the last quarter century has it been possible to identify another ideological contender potentially of the scale of the Modern Movement. This contender is the growing theory, as yet without a credible polemic, that architectural form should be derived, not so much from historical precedent or function, as from compliance with the global energetic and environmental imperatives that govern human survival. At present what these resultant architectural forms, or their definitive ideological statements will be, remains unclear. With a satisfying historical symmetry they are as enigmatic as the first white shapes of Modern Architecture must have been at the close of the 19th century.

Martin Pawley
Somerton 1999

Books
of the
Century

ONE

Pioneers

The Farman Goliath airliner, as illustrated in Le Corbusier's 1923 *Vers une Architecture*. He viewed the interplane struts metaphorically: they became columns raising the building from the ground. Source: Le Corbusier, *Vers une Architecture*, 1923.

The independent mind is not the mind of a man who can liberate himself entirely from the experiences of the past, but from the accepted intellectual categories of the present.

John Lukacs 1976

WHO OWNS FRANK LLOYD WRIGHT?

Anthony Alofsin. *Frank Lloyd Wright the Lost Years 1910–1922: A Study of Influence*. University of Chicago Press, Chicago 1993.

William Allin Storrer. *The Frank Lloyd Wright Companion*. University of Chicago Press, Chicago 1994.

Frank Lloyd Wright occupies a unique place in the architecture of the 20th century. William Allin Storrer confirms it by joining Ludwig von Kochel in devising a definitive numbering system for his master's works. Along with Wolfgang Amadeus Mozart's 'K' numbers, we now have Frank Lloyd Wright's 'S' numbers. The Storrer Index now lists 433 individual buildings and projects between 1886 and 1959. Whether it will completely supersede the older Taliesin Index, whose 'T' numbers designate projects in annual groups, remains to be seen.

In any case there is clearly vast academic mileage left in Frank Lloyd Wright, even excluding the predictable discovery of doubtful 'lost masterpieces'. After exhaustively hailing the genius of another great white male, American scholarship is now staking claim to his sources of inspiration. And here Wright is again proving fruitful, for if Anthony Alofsin is to be believed, his American talent may have been influenced by Europe after all.

In May 1939, just after Nazi Germany's occupation of Czechoslovakia, Frank Lloyd Wright paid a visit to England. His purpose was to deliver four lectures to the Royal Institute of British Architects, lectures that he supplemented by showing 16 mm colour films of life at Taliesin West, the Arizona winter home of his peripatetic architectural family. Wright had been invited to speak as a 'Modernist' in much the same way as a speaker might be invited to lecture as an 'Environmentalist' today. As far as can be discerned from the transcripts of his lectures, later published as a book and then included in Wright's own 1954 publication *The Future of Architecture*, he accepted the role of 'Modernist'. This is remarkable because from 1908 onwards he called his own architecture 'Organic Architecture' and, from the early 1930s, drew clear distinctions between it and what he came to dismiss as 'European Bauhaus Modernism'.

In that fateful spring of 1939 Frank Lloyd Wright's audiences were the largest that had ever been attracted to the new headquarters of the Royal Institute in Portland Place. The charismatic American architect drew in would-be Modernists from all over the country, young architects and students whose enthusiasm had been ignited by continental visits as well as magazine and book illustrations of the work of Le Corbusier, Walter Gropius, Ernst May, Bruno Taut, Vladimir Karfik and others.

At that time in England, 'Modernism' was conceived to be an avant garde, cosmopolitan, continental and socialistic phenomenon, with ramifications extending far beyond architectural style. All its leading figures were German, French, Italian, Czech, Soviet Russian or American. Some of the former had visited Britain, en route to the US, as refugees from Fascism. But in almost every case their visit had been brief and most English architects had never seen them. Thus the Modernists and would-be Modernists who came to hear Frank Lloyd Wright encountered their first authentic English-speaking Modern pioneer.

Wright knew Europe well for the pre-aviation age. His first visit was in 1909 and, only 2 years before the London lectures, he had passed through again on his way to the Soviet Union to inspect the enormous Collective Farms developed under Stalin's 'Five-Year Plans'. There he had seen what the émigré Russian architect Berthold Lubetkin described as:

> The disurbanization of the towns and the urbanization of the country . . . the abolition of the contradictions between the urban and the rural proletariat . . . the extinction of existing towns with their concentrated and unhealthy habitations, and their replacement with endless streams of human dwellings along the big arteries joining centres of industry with centres of agriculture.

Whether the sight of Stalin's awesome Collective Farms reminded Wright of the American Mid-West or not we do not know. What we do know is that in 1939 he had curious ideas about Europe. At one of his London lectures he assured his audience – overwhelmingly composed of young men on the brink of the last great bloodbath of the 20th century – 'The more you analyse Russian Communism, German Fascism, Italian Fascism, British democracy and American democracy, the less you will be able to see any substantial differences between them'.

Hindsight plays havoc with our perception of the inter-war years. Far from such blasé opinions being confined to out of touch non-Europeans beyond a certain age, they were widely shared. The view that another European war was out of the question was held by the whole middle and upper class, not merely in Britain but in France and America too. Wright's audiences included persons who, like himself, had attended, and voted in, a debate at the English Speaking Union on the motion 'This house believes that London is in more danger from builders than from bombers'. Support for this motion survived in certain quarters beyond the outbreak of war and lasted until the Blitz.

Frank Lloyd Wright was a 19th century man, with all that century's faith in progress. Born before Imperial Germany existed, at a time when the Emperor Napoleon III was securely on the throne of France and General Grant had just been inaugurated President of a mere 37 United States, he had seen and assimilated massive changes in his lifetime and in architectural matters considered himself far in advance of the European Modern pioneers. In one sense he was right. In 1893, the year he set up in practice on his own in Chicago, the German Modernist Mies van der Rohe was barely 7 years old, the Swiss Le Corbusier was 6 and the German Walter Gropius was 10. By 1908, when Wright's work was first featured in the American magazine *Architectural Record*, in a flamboyant article entitled 'In the Cause of Architecture', he had already designed and built 187 buildings and planned and detailed 37 more. 'In the Cause of Architecture' had compared the air-conditioned 'commercial engine' of a building that he had designed for the Larkin mail order company in Buffalo to 'an ocean liner, a locomotive or a battleship' – 14 years before any such comparisons were made by Le Corbusier. As Wright later observed: 'The words may have escaped the Swiss "discoverer" (Le Corbusier); but he was young at the time'.

Wright's 1939 London lectures tell us of his opinions on the brink of the Second World War, but they also give us a relatively early perception of his own view of his sources of inspiration. This in turn is important in considering the burden of Anthony Alofsin's book, which is that Frank Lloyd Wright was heavily influenced by the art and architecture of Europe.

This is contrary to the received wisdom that the European architectural avant garde was electrified by the publication in Berlin in 1910 and 1911 of two books devoted to Wright's work and thereby was greatly influenced by him. The next interaction. Wright's other historians and biographers agree, did not occur until 1936 when the first design of his to show European influence, the Kaufmann house, 'Falling Water', was completed.

Alofsin's view is that, in view of the small number of Wasmuth books printed in 1910 – less than 200 of the first edition – this pattern of cause and effect is unlikely. Instead he argues that Wright's visit to Europe in connection with the publication of the book was more important. Wright, he says, was welcomed in Berlin and Vienna in 1910 as a kind of American Secessionist ('The Olbrich of America') whose Chicago decorative style fitted perfectly (though by accident) into the art world of the late German and Austrian Empires.

That the work of Olbrich, Hoffmann, Wagner and Plecnik overwhelmed Wright on his European visit is not at all unlikely in view of its grand urban context, its lavishness and its cost. What Alofsin further argues is that Wright transported Secessionist detailing and imagery back to the US with him, in the form of a full-blown decorative and sculptural style of his own. A style that was destined to emerge in his work as early as Midway Gardens in 1914, then to appear in the design of accessories to the Imperial Hotel, Tokyo, and finally to form a circular planning and aperture motif that can be seen in his buildings until his death.

In many ways the interaction of European and American influences in architecture is an unrewarding study. True, European architecture was the only cultural legacy of the former American colonies. True too that it can be argued, as it was by Adolf Loos and Richard Neutra, that advanced American building technology was the mainspring of all real Modernism. But, by the same token, if iron and steel construction, lifts and skyscrapers all stemmed from Yankee ingenuity, it can still be argued that it took European Bauhaus radicalism to convert it into the bald steel and glass see-through office buildings that became the architectural calling card of the 20th century.

Drawing the line anywhere between these transatlantic stations of the cross requires an act of decision. Wright made his in the 1939 lectures by rejecting the colonial legacy to America as 'an Italo-French-English stumbling block that we still have to fight'. He ignored the European Secession (a creative movement wiped out when both its empires were overthrown in the Great War and, in any case, never more than a decorative inspiration for him), and then moved on to the inter-war Modern European urbanism advocated by the Bauhaus Modernists of the 1920s. Like Georgian architecture in America, 'Collectivized' Modernism did not appeal to him. Frank Lloyd Wright saw 'negation' at work, both in Europe's Classical heritage in America and in its inter-war preoccupations in Europe. This 'negation' was something quite unrelated to the 'affirmation' that he claimed to be expressed in his own work.

In 1939 Wright's definition of 'negation' was very simple. It encompassed any design ideology that repudiated the 'organic' connection between a building and the land upon which it stood. Thus, in Wright's view, everything from the Parthenon to the towers of Manhattan – in effect all urban projects except those of the garden city movement – were wrongly conceived. The young 'discoverer' Le Corbusier could never hope to enter Wright's 'organic' pantheon in the way that the Secessionists Olbrich and Hoffmann had. Le Corbusier was damned by his own five points of architecture, the first of which called for buildings to be raised up above ground level on columns or pilotis, thus destroying their relationship with the earth.

When Wright had arrived in Europe in 1909, as well as the decorative art of the Secession, he had found a nascent

Modernism already inextricably involved with urban ideas. Over the next 15 years, aided by the horrors of the Great War and its terminating revolutions, this strain of architectural thought came to him to seem a 'negation'. Wright had no sympathy with the European Modernists' three-dimensional metropolitan centres with their motorways, train stations, airports and masts for dirigibles incorporated into the design of office towers, factory buildings and apartment blocks. All European Modern housing was urban, as Wright saw it. Its characteristic form was the rectangular, flat-roofed 'German worker' housing of Walter Gropius and Adolf Meyer, arranged like lines of trenches.

For Wright such drastic European notions as sun angles and wind directions that determined the orientation of housing without reference to physical topography, or the most economical pattern of movement for an assembly crane used as the determining factor for the distance between rows of apartments, was wholly unacceptable. Terraced housing in principle was anathema to him. In all these things he saw architecture enacting the physical submergence of the individual into the group, and the disappearance of his own brand of 19th century individualism. In Europe, as the Czech artist Karel Teige put it, the Modern building was destined to be an instrument, not a monument. And for Wright this involved an annihilation of individuality characteristic of the mobilized slave societies of the Old World where, as the demobilized military engineer corporal Mies van der Rohe wrote in 1924: 'The individual is losing significance; his destiny is no longer what interests us. The decisive achievements in all fields are impersonal and their authors are for the most part unknown. They are part of the trend of our time towards anonymity'.

Le Corbusier's various urban plans, steadily developed from 1922 onwards into what became known as the *Ville Radieuse*, incorporated all that Wright detested. In it 'the discoverer' proposed an apartment city with a population density of 400 persons per acre housed in superblocks raised off the ground so as to leave 88 per cent of the land surface free. Later versions pushed the density up to 1200 persons per acre in 60-storey skyscrapers. In some versions Le Corbusier even addressed the possibility of mass air raids. His apartments incorporated roof slabs armoured against bombs and pilotis disposed so as to permit poison gas to blow harmlessly beneath the buildings.

This was the 'battleship existence' that Wright deplored. His American counterattack against it continued for the rest of his life. Making virtue of the enforced idleness of the Depression years, he developed, first, an Arcadian urban framework called Broadacre City and, second, a variety of building types carefully designed to fit into it. Broadacre City was designed around the principle of one acre of land per person with building plots based on household size, so that while a childless couple might have half an acre, a couple with five children would have seven acres, in effect living on a small farm. Wright also envisaged a new form of tenure whereby no one would actually own land, but only have the right to 'use and improve' it. With every household sized for self sufficiency, he reasoned, there could be no proletariat. But nor would every resident be condemned to agriculture. 'Use and Improvement' extended from the humblest residence to the spectacularly capitalistic 'Mile High Illinois' skyscraper, with its 528 storeys, outrigged helipads and 56 'atomic-powered elevators' where those inclined to be office workers would labour from 'nine to five' before driving home to their 1 and 2 acre plots.

If an endless extrapolation of Broadacre City, which emerged during Wright's lifetime in several forms from 'The Disappearing City' of 1932 to 'The Living City' of 1958, was the architects' long-term practical answer to Europe, then this in itself answers Alofsin's hypothesis. Indisputably Europe exercised an influence upon his architecture, but it was an influence that helped drive him into more and more 'Usonian' (American) solutions.

Ironically the nearest Broadacre City ever came to realization was in 1947 when, in a thoroughly American way, the Presidential Advisory Commission on Universal Military Training, concerned at the difficulty of defending the US against Soviet nuclear weapons, proposed that the whole of the habitable land surface of the country be gridded by superhighways into 25 mile squares. An industrial complex was to be located at the centre of each square, while the population would be housed in low-density linear residential zones along the highways.

An echo perhaps of the Collective Farms Wright had toured in the Soviet Union only 10 years before.

THE FATHER OF THE MODERN MUTINY: ADOLF LOOS

Kurt Lustenberger. *Adolf Loos*. Artemis Verlags, London 1994.

The definitive works on Adolf Loos have all been written, and none of them matches the power and insight of the man himself. For this reason all historians and biographers, including Kurt Lustenberger, owe a debt to the publishers of the two collections of essays 'Ins Leere gesprochen' (Spoken into the Void) 1921 and 'Trotzdem' (In spite of Everything) 1931, which embody most of Loos's prolific output of polemical and prophetic writings.

Lustenberger is late on the scene, some 60 years after the death of the great Modern pioneer, but he makes good use of the massive researches of Rukschcio and Roland Schachel, authors of the definitive Life and Work, published in 1982. For Lustenberger the full collection of Loos's projects and drawings has been given a new perspective by changed climate of architectural criticism following the post-Modern counter-revolution. Loos was seen as a foreigner and outsider during the years of the formation of the Modern ideology that culminated in the Weissenhof Exhibition of 1927 and the great 'International Style' exhibition at the Museum of Modern Art in New York in 1933. Not only was Loos refused permission to design a house for the Weissenhof exhibition curated by Mies van der Rohe – because he was deemed to be 'ideologically unsound – but after his death he was cast into the outer darkness alongside such other turn of the century individualists as Erich Mendelsohn, Hans Poelzig and Hugo Haring.

None belonged to the Corbusian 'International Front', but all had made historic contributions to the birth of Modern Architecture. Alone among them Loos had left a body of written work whose power and authority was perhaps matched only by that other outsider, and near contemporary, Frank Lloyd Wright.

Like Wright, Loos was a fearless polemicist and a devotee of the American way. Both detested academies and institutes. Both were consequently denied important official commissions until the day they died.

Adolf Loos was born in 1870 in Brno in the part of the Austro-Hungarian Empire that was destined to become Czechoslovakia in 1918. Half a generation older than Le Corbusier, Walter Gropius and Mies van der Rohe, he was a crucial figure in the emergence of utilitarian Modern thinking in Europe, and a mediator between the two worlds of commercial American architecture and the cultural avant garde of German-speaking Europe. Loos travelled to America in 1893 to visit the Chicago Exposition but stayed there for three influential years. After the Exposition he travelled to New York where he ran out of money and underwent considerable privations before at last finding work as a draughtsman. He also delayed his return to Vienna by spending several months in England on his return to Europe. Both these visits influenced him mightily, following as they did upon his abandonment of his studies at the University of Dresden and his subsequent failure to obtain entry to the Academy of Fine Arts in Vienna.

For the rest of his life, first hand knowledge of America and England fuelled Loos's dissatisfaction with German and Austrian architecture and design, and gave a sharp edge to his writings, which first attracted attention by their opposition to the dominant Secession movement. From an early stage Loos wrote extensively for weekly newspapers, using their relative freedom to bypass the conservatism of the architectural journals of the day. His seminal essay 'Ornament and Crime' was the first to equate the ornamentation of buildings with the impulse that led to criminals and prostitutes having themselves tattooed.

Loos's considerable oeuvre is overshadowed by the ideological importance of one building, the Steiner House of 1910 in Vienna, whose rear elevation is often illustrated as though it were the front, with the result cited as the first truly Modern building in Europe. Pevsner writes of it; 'Who, without being informed, would not misdate this building as the achievement of the style of 1930 completely and without any limitation'. In fact the front of the house, with its half barrel-vaulted sheet metal roof, verges on the grotesque and could easily be mistaken for a railway building. Several other Loos projects show his inability to realize the full implications of his own functionalist arguments. Only in his celebrated commercial, restaurant, shop and cafe designs did he succeed in realizing a truly Modern aesthetic early in his career. It was not until later that his houses and house projects began to attain the same authority. Notable in this regard are the Tristan Tzara house of 1925, the projected house for Josephine Baker (1927) and the masterly Muller house, built in Prague in 1930, which demonstrates his mastery of spatial liberation in the private realm.

As a short volume devoted to this enigmatic figure, Lustenberger's book is biased towards Loos's architecture rather than the essays for which the architect is best known. However as an introduction explaining both Loos's importance and his limitations, the text is excellent.

ARCHITECT OF THE CENTURY

Le Corbusier. *Towards a New Architecture*. Translated and with an introduction by Frederick Etchells. Architectural Press, London 1987.

Le Corbusier. *The City of Tomorrow*. Translated and with an introduction by Frederick Etchells. Architectural Press, London 1987.

Le Corbusier. *The Decorative Art of Today*. Translated and with an introduction by James Dunnett. Architectural Press, London 1987.

> We are living in a period of reconstruction and of adaptation to
> new social and economic conditions. In rounding this Cape Horn
> the new horizons before us will only recover the grand line of
> tradition by a complete revision of the methods in vogue and by
> the fixing of a new basis of construction fixed in logic.

So wrote the architect of the century in 1923 in that famous
collection of magazine articles that the architectural historian
Reyner Banham claims to be the only piece of architectural
writing to belong amongst the 'essential literature' of the 20th
century – *Vers une Architecture*. Typically the passage is
unclear, all we can be sure about is that it is an ultimatum, like
the rest of the book. The pictures of aeroplanes, ships and
automobiles collected by Amedee Ozenfant are clear enough
as guides for a future architecture, but what on earth does the
author mean by 'Recover the grand line of tradition'? The
more you study the passage, the more it looks like a literal
translation of the figurative French: a bad translation in fact.
Has anyone ever said that about Etchells?

Reading *Towards a New Architecture* 60 years after it was
written is a chastening experience. All the things that Le
Corbusier called for that should have happened – like an 18 m
high underground service road beneath every street – have
never come about. All the deeply unpopular things – like 'jut-
ting prows of great blocks stretching along arterial avenues,
with flats opening on every side to air and light' – have happened in abundance, but none of them has meant what he said
it would mean; and as for 'recovering the grand line of tradition', that is now being done much more literally by reverting
to the 'sunless courtyards' and 'puny trees' the master
derided.

The City of Tomorrow makes a curious reading as well.
Published the year after *Vers une Architecture* it carried on the
same pattern of ultimatums.

> In 1925, the International Exhibition of Decorative Art in Paris
> demonstrated the uselessness of any turning back to the past.
> Decorative art is dead. Modern town planning comes to birth
> with a new architecture . . . We burn our bridges and break with
> the past.

Do we indeed! What we really do is create problems for the last book in the triad, *The Decorative Art of Today*.

This time the translation by James Dunnett is new and possesses a curiously post-Modern flavour; at once glorying in the doomed political ranting of another age and at the same time unable to fully exclude an awareness of its own futility. Dunnett stabs vainly at the task of trying to make Le Corbusier sound lucid and forceful instead of hysterical, but like Etchells he fails. Indeed there are pages in the book, laden with italics and exclamation marks, that resemble nothing so much as the emphatic passages of *Mein Kampf*, which was of course written in the same year.

Untroubled by the conflict between his title, *The Decorative Art of Today*, and his own earlier announcements about the death of decorative art, Le Corbusier bulks out many pages with yet more images from Ozenfant's seemingly inexhaustible photo-file; the usual collection of bidets, door handles, briar pipes and American filing cabinets, but to no avail. The sad fact is that, even for an enthusiast, it is impossible to digest these three books without being reminded of more recent volumes on the Bermuda Triangle, or the work of New Age 'philosophers' like Erich von Daniken or Shirley Maclaine. For this reason, in the end, *The Decorative Art of Today*'s endorsement from Paul Valery, like the praise of Albert Einstein that adorns every copy of *Le Modulor*, does not help.

MORE OF MIES

Franz Schulze. *Mies van der Rohe: A Critical Biography*. University of Chicago Press, Chicago 1986.

Wolf Tegethoff. *Mies van der Rohe: The Villas and Country Houses*. MIT Press, Cambridge, MA 1986.

This month (February 1986), the New York Museum of Modern Art is holding a major exhibition to mark the centennial year of the birth of Mies van der Rohe. More than 300 drawings will be on display; eight large architectural models and two full-size mock-ups of structural details – the steel and brick corner developed for the Illinois Institute of Technology campus and the column and roof junction of the New National Gallery in Berlin. The famous chrome-steel cruciform column used in the recently reconstructed Barcelona Pavilion will be exhibited full size. This exhibition, plus the two books reviewed here, plus David Spaeth's biography last year (Architectural Press) plus the mansion House Square debacle, have conspired to thrust the work of the inscrutable modern master more clearly into the public eye in the last 12 months than at any time since his death in 1969. Whether as a symbol of all that is distasteful to the petit bourgeois, or as a reminder of all that was triumphant in modern architecture, the work of Mies refuses to be forgotten.

At a simple level the continuing presence of Mies van der Rohe in our minds is wholly explicable. He was, like Joseph Paxton or Ferdinand Porsche, the author of feats of technical virtuosity that still command the attention of designers today – in much the same way as the campaigns of Napoleon or Rommel command the attention of staff officers in the army. Some things never change, and the appeal of more for less (or less is more) is one of them. As a design imperative it is – to quote Le Corbusier – the thumb-print of the technological age. But beyond his daunting axioms there is another level at which Mies van der Rohe is interesting, and that is at the enigmatic latitude of a life understood only in its barest outlines: a career twice eclipsed and twice born again. It is here that Schulze's book makes its major and probably unrepeatable contribution, for it is unlikely that a better combination of intelligence and scholarship will be brought to bear during the lifetimes of the remaining protagonists.

From Schulze we learn, in addition to the broad outline of Mies' life, such fascinating details as the fact that his 1910 competition entry for the Bismarck monument was a photomontage – a full decade before his better known use of this technique. We learn that he thought Berlage a more 'modern' architect than Behrens and that he wanted to include his neo-Classic Kroller house project in a Bauhaus exhibition in 1919 but

Gropius vetoed it. Of his military service in the Great War we gain a curiously Sergeant Bilko-like impression; with frequent spells of sick leave and clerical work at regimental headquarters in Berlin finally terminated by a dismal field assignment 'guarding railway sidings' in Romania. In the same way his famous gloomy utterances, such as the often quoted sentence beginning 'The individual is losing significance . . .', are unerringly traced to the annotated and well thumbed volumes of Spengler found in his library. Similarly his enthusiasm for America is rooted in Walter Rathenau – 'Nothing since the Middle Ages is as imposing as New York City' – and not in the experience of motopia, for he never learned to drive, even though he owned a second-hand Oldsmobile when he died in 1969.

Tegethoff's book, at twice the price, is an altogether more conventional architectural volume. Based on an earlier Mies exhibition held at the Kaiser Wilhelm Institute in Krefeld, West Germany, it contains a multitude of original photographs and drawings, as well as an intense discussion of 'the spatial needs of modern man' – the latter being the author's interpretation of Mies's quest as a designer. Two major elements are deep studies of the reinforced concrete and the brick country house projects of the 1920s. The evolution of these projects into the completed Tugendhat House, the Barcelona Pavilion, the Resor House project and the Farnsworth House is meticulously followed. The latter two offer a remarkable insight into the real meaning of less is more, for Farnsworth is to be seen *within* the clumsy and grandiloquent Resor design. With all the South Fork elements removed it emerges naked and unashamed 10 years later.

ANATOMY OF A CONTRADICTORY MAN

John Allan. *Berthold Lubetkin: Architecture and the Tradition of Progress*. RIBA, London 1992.

On the cover of this massive volume is an almost abstract photograph of the penguin pool at Regent's Park Zoo. It is Berthold Lubetkin's best known work and in many ways a symbol of the era of his greatest achievements, the innocent age of Modernism that ended with the Blitz. But to see the elegant interlocking ramps of this 60-year old sculpture and to understand the mind of its designer are two different things.

Berthold Lubetkin was born in Imperial Russia in 1901 and died in Bristol, England, in 1990. Before he was 30 he had survived a revolution, a civil war, an exodus, an odyssey and a migration that are part of a history that few Europeans can now remember. After the age of 30 his career as a socialist architect, mostly in England, was brilliantly successful, but it lasted barely 20 years. After the fall of the post-war Labour government, he drifted into a kind of semi-retirement that was rather like the house arrest of a Soviet dissident. He returned triumphantly 30 years later, like a wrongly imprisoned innocent, to become a glittering architectural celebrity during the last decade of his life.

The author of this book, himself an architect, spent 20 years talking to and compiling material on this man and most of what he found out is somewhere in this enormous book. As a smaller photograph on the inside of the jacket reveals – Allan seated above and behind Lubetkin, loosely protective left arm framing the old man's shoulders – the relationship between the two must have been unassailable. No more definitive or compendious volume will ever be written. Virtually everything that is known of Lubetkin – apart from that which can be gleaned from his surviving buildings, all of which are Listed, some Grade 1 (the same rank as Saint Paul's cathedral) – is to be found somewhere in these pages, along with a bibliography, extracts from his speeches, drawings of every building he designed and a print of virtually every photograph of him that survives.

Yet despite Allan's industry and affection for his subject, Lubetkin remains an enigma and, in the end, a surprisingly unrewarding one. He emerges as a man who, despite his own best efforts at writing himself into history, never broke out of the mind set of the 1930s and has surprisingly little to convey to present day architects, except a reputation for courage and wit – both double-edged weapons at best.

In Britain, Lubetkin's work, his sharp words and his reputation have long been used by architectural polemicists as a club to beat fogeys, fashionableness and bureaucracy. Now bureaucracy takes its revenge, for there is a rich irony in the fact that this book is published by the Royal Institute of British Architects, an organization Lubetkin himself dismissed as 'cynically wielding patronage, distributing fringe benefits to approved hacks, and bestowing titles on safe creeps groomed for eminence in the gloom of committee rooms'.

As far as the 'tradition of progress' of the title is concerned, there is not as much evidence of it as might be expected. For example in 1987, when he was 86 years old, the following exchange between Lubetkin and the architectural historian Gavin Stamp was published in the *Architects' Journal*.

Stamp   Many people think my affection for old telephone kiosks is silly, but they were actually an authoritative design.

Lubetkin   Yes it was a positive design, something which was wanted because it was right.

Stamp   Had BT commissioned a new, good modern design I would have no complaint.

Lubetkin   But who is to do it now? There is so little talent about.

Little talent perhaps, but a lot of progress. The wisdom of these two, their ages separated by 40 years but each as innocent as the other of the advance of the cellular telephone, perhaps illuminates Lubetkin's failings as a visionary. After the passing of the age of socialist public housing, he was lost. From then on, more often than not, it was only his splendidly savage wit that disguised the lack of rigour in his thinking and his blithe disregard for glaring contradictions. Thus Prince Charles was a 'pub-crawling populist' one minute and 'behaving like Stalin' the next. The great Frank Lloyd Wright was 'a clown'. Le Corbusier's chapel at Ronchamp was 'a Punch and Judy show almost as bad as the new National Gallery extension'.

When he really got into gear during his years of stardom, Lubetkin gorged himself on contradictions. Not only did his recorded contempt for the RIBA not prevent him from dining regularly with the Institute's secretary, but his admiration for progress did not prevent him from seeing the high-tech architects of the 1980s – who might be supposed to be the natural successors to such pre-war Moderns as himself – as 'awful'. Richard Rogers' Lloyd's building he dismissed as 'mechanical materialism, judged simply by calculating the number of bolts'. In the same way Community Architecture was 'no more than a fiction. Who is the authority to consult? Chaps in the street? They obviously don't know'.

The post-Modernists – who might possibly have hoped for some encouragement on the basis of the peculiar caryatids supporting the porch of Lubetkin's famous Highpoint flats – found themselves dismissed as 'Hepplewhite and Chippendale in drag'. And they were lucky to get off so lightly. Prince Charles's beloved New Classicists had to endure worse: 'There may be no law against impersonating your grandmother – it's just that you don't'.

Recounting examples of Berthold Lubetkin's savage wit is a fine way to pass the time and Allan's book is a treasure trove of it. But at the deeper level of human personality, it fails. Somehow the real Lubetkin, who lurked nihilistically behind his building, his politicking and his wit, remains immured in them forever.

LITTLE AND LARGE

Malcolm Reading and Peter Coe. *Lubetkin and Tecton: An Architectural Study*. Triangle Architectural Publishing, London 1993.

For a man born in the second year of the present century, who virtually retired from architectural practice in the 1950s, Berthold Lubetkin is remarkable in his power to exert more fascination after his death than he did while he was still alive. In addition to John Allan's mammoth biography, privately printed collections of his writings and transcripts of his lectures continue to circulate, and the demand for them increases.

Malcolm Reading and Peter Coe's small but authoritative book represents a sort of half-way house between these two poles of Lubetkiniana: better organized than the *Samizdat* writings of the architect himself, but in most ways unequal to Allan's monster work, not least in the matter of profusion of illustrations. Nonetheless, at a price less than one-third of that of the authorized biography, this book represents a necessary investment.

The early chapters provide a very readable and objective account of the peripatetic life of the architect of the famous Penguin Pool. If there is a general weakness, it is the same as Allan's – a grim determination to maintain a level of seriousness about life, the universe and everything that the architect himself did not generally convey to those he met.

An interesting insight that emerges from the book is the way that critics and commentators have tended to judge the pre-war housing schemes for Finsbury Council by Lubetkin and Tecton on the basis of their belated post-war realization. In fact, as Reading and Coe point out, projects like the Busaco Street flats (completed as the Priory Green Estate by Skinner and Bailey after Tecton's dissolution) were actually far more advanced in their 1937 incarnation. Like Finsbury Health Centre, with its pioneer service ducts and open planning, Lubetkin's pre-war mass housing boasted very high amenity standards. At Busaco Street, high-density, subsidized slum-clearance council flats, costed well within current limits, were intended to have individual entrances from lifts and stairwells; to be equipped with Garchey water-borne waste disposal systems; separate bathrooms and WCs; central heating; a communal laundry, nursery and clinic. Beneath the extensive green area between the long four and eight storey blocks, there was also to have been a deep spiral underground car park that would have served as an air raid shelter in the event of war. When this scheme was finally built, virtually all these features were abandoned for reasons of cost. It is in such details that the reader begins to see the sources of the disillusion that led Lubetkin to abandon the practice of architecture in disgust.

Although the idea of Lubetkin as a theorist of reason and objectivity is not really reconcilable with the work of Lubetkin the architect, there is a poignancy in the failure of the cash-strapped, post-war Socialist utopia to match up to Lubetkin's reasonable expectations of it. Perhaps his finest monument in this regard is his recorded opposition, late in his life, to the extravagant Listing of his surviving buildings. This he opposed, as Reading and Coe point out, because the buildings *were crying out for a world that had never come into being.*

THE HOUSE: A MACHINE FOR LIVING IN

Anthony Bertram. *The House: A Machine for Living In.*
A & C Black, London 1935.

'This book is for the layman – a popular book, as it is called – but I will try to avoid making it a book for half-wits.' So begins Anthony Bertram's *The House: A Machine for Living In*, a masterpiece published in 1935, never reprinted, but undoubtedly my best read of 1985 even though it cost me £8.50 from Inch's instead of 1s 6d had I been quicker off the mark.

Bertram was one of those people as utterly convinced of the virtues of modern architecture then as the junta at SAVE are about the qualities of anything built before 1914 today. Such certainty is always wonderful to read, anywhere from *Private Eye* to the letters column of *The Times*. Try this:

> Not only have the methods exploited in 1851 by Paxton been neglected, but long-discarded techniques have been revived and misused to satisfy the ignorant whims of amateurs of ye old picturesque. The deal laths on Tudoresque villas are the most tremendous symbols of the architectural rottenness which has infested most people in this Middle-Ages-ridden country. Useless, meaningless, tawdry and yet costing good money . . .

And so on and on, in the chapter after chapter dealing with the 'chassis' of the house, heating and ventilating – 'We have more respect for our healths than our carpets' – everything that can and should be said about design, all written in the blessed age before the £300 billion resale housing market turned the 'machines for living in' into 'investments for living in' and their design into three-dimensional stocks and bonds.

THE FULLER FIGURE

Lloyd Steven Sieden. *Buckminster Fuller's Universe: An Appreciation*. Plenum Press, New York 1989.

Just why Richard Buckminster Fuller's influence should still be burgeoning years after his death at the age of 88 is an open question. Though best known as a philosopher, mathematician and designer, he was also a sometime professor of poetry and perhaps one of the most prolific public speakers ever to remain outside politics. According to the Buckminster Fuller Institute in Los Angeles he gave over 1000 lectures at 544 educational institutions between 1945 and 1983, and managed 120 speaking engagements in his peak year. A Royal Gold Medallist for Architecture himself, the week before he died Fuller delivered the oration at his protege Norman Foster's Royal Gold Medal ceremony.

Marathon lectures and weighty tomes apart, Fuller is famous for three pieces of hardware: the mast-supported Dymaxion House; the aircraft-style rear steering, Dymaxion car and the geodesic dome. The first of these was never built; the second existed only in hair-raising prototype form – three were built and only one survives – and the third was an unqualified production success. Between 1954 and 1971 no less than 300 000 geodesic domes and spheres were built before Fuller's master patent expired, including the famous US pavilion at EXPO 67.

Sieden's story of Fuller's life is long and detailed but also very indulgent. Interesting though unsavoury episodes like his disgrace at Harvard, his shotgun marriage and his sacking by the Celotex Corpation are either ignored or not explored. His 1927 breakdown is presented as more of a creative ferment. Historically important matters, like the glaring disparity between the grotesque '4-D' patent application house design of 1928 and the 1932 'Dymaxion' model that has passed into the history books with the date '1927', are not examined. The circumstances attending the accident that destroyed Dymaxion car number one are fudged; while whether car number two or car number three is the one that is preserved remains unclear (to Sieden). The way in which Fuller's own stubbornness led to the collapse of his housebuilding company in 1946 – a collapse that disappointed millions and discredited the whole prefabrication industry in America – is glossed over. A curtain too is drawn over the precise contribution, and in some cases the fate, of gifted collaborators and students like Starling Burgess, Kenneth Snelson, Don Richter, Tom Moore, Peter Pearce and many more, without whose work Fuller's achievements might never have come about.

In the years since he died on a hospital visit to his wife Anne, herself to die 36 hours later, Fuller has become a cult figure. This immensely readable book is not so much biography or scholarship as a part of that process.

TWO

Revivalists

What was the joke? Leon Krier introduces architect John Thompson to Prince Charles on the site of his future Potemkin village at Poundbury. Source: Author's collection.

> *People do not remember. The institutionalized machines of oblivion are running at full speed, image machines, calculators. It is therefore necessary to repeat. People work through repetition until they remember. Only in this manner do they arrive at the critical Archimedean point where one can read the sentence 'The more past, the more future', and understand it.*
>
> Dietmar Kamper 1994

PRINCE VALIUM

Charles Jencks. *The Prince, the Architects, and New Wave Monarchy*. Academy Editions, London 1988.

Once long ago in the 1960s the Prince Consort, Prince Philip, the husband of the Queen of England, decided that the Royal Estates at Sandringham were decrepit and out of date. Apparently without the opposition of the Queen he hired a Cambridge architect, a Modernist named David Roberts, to demolish the old stuff and design a new house. In the 1960s this was all the rage, the Duke of Westminster had already had his family home razed to the ground and replaced by a brutalist concrete palazzo designed by his son-in-law John Dennys. But Prince Phillip's initiative came to nought. Conservative forces within the Royal Household spoke up in favour of old Victorian brick Sandringham and a safe pair of hands in the shape of Sir Hugh Casson replaced Roberts. A little light refurbishment was carried out instead.

Charles Jencks apparently does not know of this story, which is a pity, for he desperately needed it and more like it to bulk out this trite and obsolescent little book. Today Philip's son and hier to the throne, Prince Charles Philip Arthur George Windsor (*b.* 1948), is also interested in architecture, but of a different kind. A trained helicopter pilot and once the commander of a little warship when he was in the Navy, Charles is a serious fellow. Unlike his reputedly reformed sister he has never been caught by a police pursuit car cannonballing down the motorway to Gloucestershire. Nor – unlike his former wife – has he ever frequented a night club dressed up in police uniform. Charles believes in traditional values and likes old things, especially old buildings and everything that goes with them. He is the epitome of the character in the Monty Python sketch who dreads coming into contact with anything 'tinny'.

Charles is bored by the modern world with its mobile telephones, security guards and chattering fax machines. He has made a career out of his distaste for all its manifestations. He hates modern buildings. He hates modern medicine. He hates not having any power. He knows that, modern medicine being what it is, he stands a good chance of still being plain old Prince Charles at the turn of the century. And so, from time to time, he gets cross.

In the last 5 years he has expressed forceful views on trade with Australia, homeopathic medicine, inner city aid, marine archaeology, dyslexia, Aids, the German Officer Corps and the Luftwaffe, adventure training, business efficiency, and, most recently, the media. On September 15th 1988, for example, he amazed an audience of dignitaries at the opening of a 'Museum of the Moving Image' in London by exploding 'It is palpable nonsense to say that violence on TV has no effect on people's behaviour. The people who say this are so-called experts who attempt to confuse ordinary people so they feel they do not know what they are talking about!'.

This outburst embodied the one perception that the prince has brought to all the fields that have engaged his attention. Four years earlier he had famously berated an equally amazed audience of architects at Hampton Court with the almost identical accusation that:

> For far too long architects have consistently ignored the feelings and wishes of the mass of ordinary people in this country . . . Architects and planners do not necessarily have the monopoly of knowing best about taste, style and planning . . . Ordinary people should not be made to feel guilty or ignorant if their natural preference is for more traditional designs.

Everywhere in the modern world, it seems, there are 'so-called experts' telling 'ordinary people' what to do and he, or rather one, has had enough of it.

Despite all this indignation expressed over the years, extending from his bizarre performance at the now famous question and answer session at Harvard GSD, through the scandalous succession of outbursts in England about 'carbuncles', 'glass stumps', 'hardened missile silos' and 'Victorian prisons', right up to the much lauded Pittsburgh conference speech, Prince Charles has showed no sign of accumulating a grasp of the realities of architectural practice. Like the Bourbons before him he learns nothing and forgets nothing. A state of affairs that may owe much to his choice of advisers – a bizarre collection of New Georgian magazine editors who dress up in 18th century clothes; messianic university lecturers, interior designers, property developers and reactionary newspaper columnists – none of whom have any grasp of these realities either. No matter, ignorance has not stopped their monothematic protege from becoming established as the foremost arbiter of popular taste in the land. Today where architecture is concerned – at least until he himself loses interest in it – Prince Charles is the champion of all philistines, the denouncer of vile professional expertise, the embodiment of the man in the street. When in 1987 he appeared to volunteer to retire from public life – 'I don't need to do all this . . . If people would rather I did nothing about it, I will go off somewhere . . . I sometimes wonder why I don't pack it in an spend my time playing polo' – a swift public opinion poll assured him that a 76 per cent sample wanted him to go on just, going on.

Charles Jencks has lived in Prince Charles's realm for many years. Unlike Charles Windsor, Charles Jencks does not hate the modern world, in fact he so adores its twists and turns that, as did Napoleon the sons of his favourite soldiers, he christens them himself. Over the last 20 years names of movements and tendencies have tripped from his pen, typewriter and finally word processor until the entire history of 20th century architecture can be explored without ever leaving the lush garden of his prose. In the nature of things it was inevitable that the future King's dalliance with architecture would lead Charles and Charles to meet, and that the one should forthwith begin to weave the other into his rich tapestry of wasms and isms.

What cannot have been inevitable, at least at first, was that Jencks would make such a thin, hagiographical mess of this opportunity to touch the crown of ages. Clearly Charles the writer was overawed by Charles the future King. Certainly at a debate on the subject of Prince Charles and Architecture held at the Tate Gallery in 1989 to coincide with the publication of his book, Jencks surprised his audience by announcing that its Right Royal subject matter was so delicate that he was unable to depart from a written text and could answer no questions.

This may have made putative readers more curious about the thin sliver of a book itself, but it cannot have done so for long. *The Prince, the Architects, and New Wave Monarchy* is a dogged and old-fashioned study in pop sociology, a genre that requires above all that sureness of touch with the social hierarchy that an expatriate can never possess. Thus we have Jencks, no longer lightly hopping from neologistic conceit to neolgistic conceit, but lumbering along in the wake of the gossip columnists and 'style commentators' who have already done to death every possible comparison between the Royals and the Soaps, Windsor and Hollywood. His one invention, the acronym 'PADS' for 'Planners, Architects and Developers', succeeds only in aping the misconceptions of his Prince by bundling together a squabbling trio whose work and destiny is better understood apart. But in the end worse even than this book's ephemerality – what after all could be more ephemeral than the grovelling tale of an hereditary Prince's fleeting interest in something that he thought was simple, like sketching, but turned out to be complicated and boring in the end – is the way in which its length has had to be made up, not by scholarship, but by a bundle of reprinted newspaper articles about Charles's speeches, all carefully chosen for their servile tone. This, for the man who invented post-Modernism, is surely the bottom of the lowest barrel of all.

THOSE FABULOUS KRIER BROTHERS

Leon Krier. *Architecture and Urban Design.* Academy Editions, London 1993.

Rob Krier. *Architecture and Urban Design.* Academy Editions/Ernst & Sohn, London 1994.

Hmmm. Heft these two books! Quite something eh? Did you ever see the two Krier brothers together? I did. It was at one of Papa Doc's seances at the Royal Academy. There they sat,

Rob and Leo, judiciously apart in the crowd, both smiling confidently for all the world as though they were directors of the Bank of European Reconstruction and Development which, in a manner of speaking, I suppose they were. But who could imagine in that headquarters of the artistic establishment that, only a quarter of a century before, they had been penniless unknowns, architectural castaways on an ocean of Modernism, prey to the most dubious associations and seemingly most unlikely to rise to their present heights of power and influence.

The rise of the Krier brothers is a parable of our times. It proves lots of things. It proves fractal geometry (same shapes, different scales), it proves catastrophe theory (twist things enough and the whole mental structure reverses), it proves the asymptotic nature of the universe (everything converges, nothing ever meets), it proves Hegelian dialectics (everything tends towards its opposite), and of course it proves the eventual popularity of unpopularity, the power-packed punch of Princes and ascendancy of fame over actual achievement . . . Yes, the success of the Krier's proves lots of things. Not least that, provided you have a lot of drawings to show, the voyage from architectural obscurity to the innermost fastnesses of the establishment can be so quick you don't actually have to build anything at all.

The Krier brothers were born in Luxembourg around the end of World War Two. Rob before and Leo after the Battle of the Bulge. Unbeknownst to them, this historical accident was destined to make a profound impression. Being conservative Luxemburgers their family was effectively neutral during the war and so, to this day, the brothers both sport a kind of Hemingwayish war correspondent manner and draw Third Mannish drawings for their clients. In their mind set there are always barrage balloons overhead, drunken Americans in jeeps sacking castles on the Rhine, aircraft droning menacingly overhead and picturesquely impoverished aristocrats selling themselves amongst the ruins for a cheese sandwich. A postmortem performed on the pair of them would probably find the date 1945 chiselled on their hearts. For them it was not only the year their own clock started, but the year the clock of real European civilization stopped. They have both worked like Stakhanovites ever since, trying to start it up again and reinstate the old Europe shattered by the Pax Americana. Their dream is to put Europe back together again without Marx or Lenin, or Le Corbusier, or Mies van der Rohe, McDonalds, Safeway, Video, Boeing and T-shirts.

Despite being older than his brother, and having more actual built work to show, Rob's is the slighter of these two books. An alleged Modernist in his early years, the elder Krier looks distinctly proto-Swedish-pomo in the designs shown here. From the outset he had problems with massing and, as time passed and bigger opportunities came along, this evolved into a game of deliberate disproportion. Thus small houses with a vast column or two soon led to big urban designs with punched out lightwells and 1945-style bombed Romanesque skylines. Rob never got into elaborate renderings the way his brother did. Their convergence – by the late 1980s Rob seemed more and more to be sketching what Leo would later magnify into epic coloured scenes – took a more subtle form. True, Rob tried his hand at Leo's forte, Classical revival resort architecture, but mostly he stuck to planning quarters in European cities. The best picture in either book is a delightful 1991 shot of both brothers in Pforzheim, dressed like merchant bankers and clearly in full agreement, sharing a joke at the foot of a recently bombed statue by Rob.

Apart from a generic publishing house design resemblance, Leo's family bible-sized tome is quite different. How the wild-haired Leo, New Georgian cult figure of 1980s London, ever became a Florida resort designer, the first and only longhand masterplanner of Spitalfields, and the drafter of the Prince of Wales's vision of the 'Greater Dorchester', is an interesting question but, despite a lavish 300 pages it does not get answered here. There is little autobiographical detail in either volume, and Leo's, with 'over 2000 drawings', offers least of all: an extremely short introduction in which he draws a sardonic parallel between the '45 000 Allied bullets' it took to 'kill one German soldier in World War Two', and the '10 000 architectural drawings' it took him over the last 25 years to achieve the building of 'a small house, three podiums for sculptures and planning permission for a small town'.

REARGUARD ACTION

Roger Scruton. *The Classical Vernacular: Architectural Principles in an Age of Nihilism*. Carcanet Press, London 1994.

The Czech philosopher Vilem Flusser (1920–1991) once wrote an essay about anachronism in the consciousness of individual human beings. In it he claimed that it was possible to walk down a modern street and pass a Neolithic man, a 21st century man, a Victorian woman, a Medieval woman or an 18th century man, all in the space of a few minutes. Reading this selection of essays by Roger Scruton is an experience that puts one in mind of Flusser, for Scruton resembles nothing so much as an 18th century man at large in late 20th century England.

In his writing, Roger Scruton conveys the impression of being bemused and perplexed by the world of nihilism in which he finds himself, but only occasionally made angry by it. For the most part he observes it much as Captain Bligh must have regarded the antics of the natives of Tahiti, with a kind of grim tolerance. In one of the best essays in the book, Scruton describes a dinner at the Royal College of Art held in connection with a Thatcher-inspired government seminar on 'Design'. He evokes this grotesque meeting of nihilistic and political minds with Joycean skill and remembers his despair when a junior minister insists that, if only British Design were better, everything we made could be sold to Japan!

In a wonderful evocation of the period, Scruton describes himself looking around the Brutalist 1960s Royal College interior for some 'British-designed' object that might conceivably interest a Japanese. His eyes alight on only one thing, a Georgian silver candlestick. Not at all what the minister had in mind, but perfect for Scruton to make his point about the futility of 'Design' as conceived by the Thatcherites.

Scruton's meditation on a candlestick is one of a number of brilliant rearguard actions fought in this collection, all of them acts of defiance against the encircling nihilistic gloom, and most of them written 10 years or more ago. Today they will cut no ice with the ozone layer crowd. Daft as 'Design' may have been in the 1980s, it was nothing like as scary as it is now, with its seminars given over to banning washing machines because of their benzene fumes, banning cars from cities, banning shopping from the countryside, banning air conditioning, and plastering buildings with solar cells instead of columns and pediments. Today our magnificent 18th century man would be lucky if the worst that happened to him was that he were cast adrift in an open boat.

Once professor of Aesthetics at Birkbeck College, Roger Scruton is now a professor at Boston University. There, in the American Academic Northeast, he has inherited the mantle of another English emigre, the architecture critic Colin Rowe. Like Scruton, Rowe has a low opinion of schools of architecture. While in one of his essays Scruton blames them for turning Modernism from 'a harmless eccentricity' into 'an educational programme linked to international socialism and other ill-considered projects for the moral regeneration of mankind', Rowe comes even more swiftly to the point. In a recent issue of the magazine *Architecture New York* he described architectural education as, 'After the Russian Revolution, the two world wars, the Holocaust and Modern architecture itself, the greatest catastrophe of the 20th century'.

Naturally Rowe contributed to this 'catastrophe'. So did Scruton, who has been marinated in 'educational programmes' for years, whether he likes them or not. As he savages his Modernist villains in his old-fashioned way, he seems unconscious of the irony of his own position, translated from 18th century visitor to ghost. Walter Gropius, Le Corbusier, Mies van der Rohe, Manfredo Tafuri, Richard Buckminster Fuller . . . All his diabolical figures are dead. In the whole book of essays no victim ever replies.

TODAY, YES, BUT WHAT ABOUT TOMORROW?

David Pearce. *Conservation Today*. Routledge, London 1989.

It is interesting that nobody seems to have any compunction these days about calling conservation an 'industry'. Perhaps, in the de-industrialized state of contemporary Britain, this is not surprising. Since we have ceased to manufacture anything except debt, and ceased to have anything to sell except oil and a few Jaguars, conservation might as well be an industry as 'financial services', 'invisible exports' (another post-Modern invention), and 'exhibiting your grandmother's corpse for money' – as Henry James described the tourist industry in Rome.

Not that David Pearce is much troubled by doubt. For him the triumph of conservation over the philistines has been something of a personal crusade, not dissimilar to holding the pass at Thermopylae or the Battle of Britain. The dismal statistics that show just how little investment is going into new buildings and infrastructure these days are to him giant 'V' signs that show how conservation has triumphed over the bulldozer. Half the annual construction budget involves work on existing buildings; half the work of the architectural profession is 'rehabilitation' and more people visit historic buildings than go to the cinema. Case proven. We hardly need the 11 introductory pages of polemic, exposing 'the failure of the idea that once everyone is provided with decent, standardized accommodation they will live happily and peaceably in collective harmony'. Pearce has an answer to that one. 'They don't. They urinate in the lifts'.

One could say that such Charles III thinking pervades the whole of *Conservation Today* but actually most of the book consists not of argument – nobody of consequence ever opposed conservation – but of 'case histories' in which picturesque ruins become antique shops, picture galleries and tastefully lower case McDonalds. Truly, as Pearce quotes the Central Policy Studies Unit, our heritage earns more than our motor industry, but somebody else called Hewison has already written a book about that (*The Heritage Industry*, Methuen, London 1987).

All that was left for Pearce and the RFAC consortium to do was to put together an exhibition at the Royal Academy and a catalogue masquerading as a book that more or less says that architects, clients and local government have all come to their senses since 1975 and now everything is alright and getting better and better. 'We should be aware of our good fortune in being alive in an age when we can sit in front of a log fire in a 17th century hearth, listening to compact discs while eating food prepared in kitchens equipped with spin-offs from space-age technology', concludes Pearce. This, he freely concedes, has nothing to do with the past. It is to do with the future. What an industry conservation is!

IN TOUCH WITH THE INFINITE

HRH the Prince of Wales and Charles Clover. *Highgrove: Portrait of an Estate*. Chapmans 1992.

Prince Charles is, as everyone knows, a reticent man who only appears in print or on television with the greatest reluctance. Thus we learn with surprise from the first paragraph of his short introduction to this glossy volume that he has been bombarded with requests to write books and make films about Highgrove ever since he took over the old place, but he has always refused to allow anything of the kind.

Always that is until a commercial television company made him an offer he could not refuse.

'I should have known', the Prince writes knowingly, 'that what started as a film would very soon develop into a suggestion to produce a book'. Of course 'He could never find the time to write an entire book himself', but he knew a man who could, Charles Clover, Environment Editor of the *Daily Telegraph*, who is 'an agnostic about organic farming methods'.

Between them, Clover and Windsor have produced this vast and heavily illustrated volume, with Clover doing the bulk of the writing, industriously boiler plating his text with much potted local and architectural history, and a minor compendium of information about plants, beasts of the fields, tractors, nitrogen, phosphates and ammonia. At the end of it, as befits a loyal subject, Charles Clover has become a convinced organicist, enthusing over what Charles Windsor calls his 'sewage garden', an organic complex of ponds and pipes that not only disposes of faeces, but yields a crop of reeds for 'basket-weaving' as well as nourishing the water-plants 'that Miriam Rothschild considers best for a dragonfly reserve'. In his turn Charles too is mellowed by the creative experience, confessing that he has come to understand the problems faced by all farmers from Ladakh to Chippenham, but promising them that they will 'feel in control' and 'come to feel like farmers again' once they adopt organic methods.

If all this is only to be expected in what will now opportunely serve as a promotional book for the more seemly side of the Prince's exciting life, the unexpected part of *Highgrove: The Portrait of an Estate* is the extent to which it is dominated by the idea of an autonomous country retreat. Despite Charles's exclamation mark-strewn disclaimers, one of them even dismissing the book's own title ('To call Highgrove an estate is, I think, stretching a point a bit too far!'), the eponymous 300-acre spread emerges as no ordinary country seat. After we have absorbed the accumulated wisdom of Charles's advisors – the apparent polymath Lady Salisbury, the seer Wendell Berry, the aforementioned expert on wildflowers Miriam Rothschild, the 'horseman and survivor' Paddy Whiteland, the stonemason Fred Ind, the 'very special man' Cecil Gardiner, the furniture maker John Makepeace, and so on – it is clear that this house is not only in daily contact with 'those wise traditions which form mankind's lifeline with the profoundly mysterious laws of the universe', but also combines the characteristics of a Swiss clinical laboratory and a national monument.

Just how Highgrove attained this status is interesting. Not many years ago it was the monastery that was the amateur's paradigm of rural autarchy. There Monks were summoned by bells and ancient carp hovered in limpid pools in a universe not merely governed by the rules of a religious order, but synchronized with a natural order too, from which it derived its own ecological balance. But then came the dissolution of the Monasteries and this image faded away to be replaced by a profane successor, the country house.

In the 19th century, even after the coming of the railways, country estates were still being laid out cheek by jowl across the English landscape like monster suburban gardens. The myth is that they were autarchic settlements of an enlightened type. In fact they burned hundreds of tons of Newcastle coal a year and required armies of servants on starvation wages to sustain their feudal grandeur. Literature, through various subplots, all faithfully turned from novels into moving pictures and then serialized on TV, has faithfully charted the progress of these rural battle cruisers from Tom Jones to Mansfield Park and then to Brideshead. At Brideshead the lure of the country bogged down for a time – no one respectable knew what to make of its not at all healthy mixture of grandeur and decay – and after 1945 the rot really set in. More and more country houses were turned into preparatory schools, conference centres or flats, and rendered even more disreputable by association Americans, cults and Profumo-style scandals.

It is not too much to say that Highgrove came along just in time to prevent the final collapse of the country house ideal. The country house myth needed Prince Charles as much as he needed a country house myth and, when he got hold of Highgrove and welded it onto the tail end of a great wave of New Age vegetarian codswallop, both were magically reborn. Soon there was no more need for talk of serfs and paupers, starving labourers tugging at their forelocks, snarling squires or brutal masters of hounds. With the advent of Highgrove the country house ceased to be a sociological phenomenon and became instead something to do with The Environment.

Whether Prince Charles can establish a new identity as a farmer on the strength of this record of his eco-antics at Highgrove may be open to question, but legion suburbanites will find his sentimental devotion to flora, fauna, sewage systems and amateur expertise far more palatable than the huntin', shootin' and fishin' style of his forebears.

THREE

Dictators

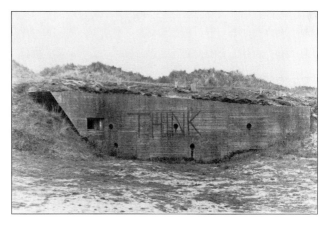

A World War Two German bunker on the island of Jersey, with appropriate graffiti, photographed in 1970. Source: Author.

The essence of Fascism is the power of adaptation to fresh facts. Above all, it is a realist creed. It has no use for immortal principles in relation to the facts of bread and butter; and it despises the windy rhetoric which ascribes importance to mere formulae. The steel creed of an iron age, it cuts through the verbiage of illusion to the achievement of a new reality.

Oswald Mosley 1932

STRONG STUFF THIS CLASSICISM

Peter Adam. *The Arts of the Third Reich.*
Thames & Hudson, London 1990.

In the old days we used to believe that Classicism was discredited by its association with the evils of Nazism: that was why Modernism emerged triumphant after World War Two. Then came a second theory: that the reason everything went wrong in Europe between 1933 and 1945 was not because of Classicism, but because Classicism got into the wrong hands. Powerful stuff, like plutonium, it gave its evil masters almost supernatural powers. It took a World War just to get Classicism back into safe hands. In recent years, and especially since Prince Charles's speeches exculpating the German Officer Corps and the Luftwaffe, this 'Raiders of the Lost Ark' theory of Classicism has swept the board. Now we all accept that a Classical building is only as good or bad as the man who pays for it.

The two BBC documentaries on the art of the Third Reich that Peter Adam made in 1988 formed the basis of this book, and it is interesting to see that the merits and the defects of the television programmes are transported into the book without alteration. I recall watching Adam's television programmes with mixed feelings: on the one hand, admiration for his archival finds and editing skill, and, on the other, mounting rage at the pretence that he seemed determined to maintain, that no other political regime had ever employed the arts in the manner of the Nazis. Running into him at the BBC one day, I questioned him about this. His reply was that the omission of comparisons was intentional. Adam believed that it was the task of the viewer to supply any such comparisons and reach his or her own conclusions about the presence or absence of government 'Arts management' elsewhere and at other times.

Four years later the effect of the lack of comparisons in the book is even more disturbing than it was on the screen. Somehow it succeeds in magnifying the phenomenon of Nazi art even as it dismisses its quality. Despite the overwhelming output of images thrown up by his massive researches Adam repeatedly assures us that all the art of the III Reich was 'inferior', 'second rate', 'derivative', 'corrupt', 'boring', 'simplistic'. . . So much so that finally the reader rebels. Was Hitler's regime really worse in this respect than those of Stalin, Franco or Ceausescu? Was the Nazi exploitation of the composition and technique of Renaissance paintings any more corrupt than its subsequent plundering by the advertising industry, exposed by John Berger in his seminal 'Ways of Seeing'? Were Troost, Tessenow, Sagebiel, Bonatz, Kreis and Speer really just second rate architects? The reader must make up his or her own mind – as Adam would no doubt say – but the weight and mass of the imagery of the book leaves little room for doubt. The endless fascination that must have powered Adam's researches, the pain that must have accompanied his access to so few colour pages, all of this is obvious. Even as he hurls insults at his subject matter, its sheer volume betrays the author's obsession. Like it or not, this is for him the real creative phenomenon of the 20th century. The lingering impression left by *The Arts of the Third Reich* is that their grip upon at least one creative brain has not been exorcised yet.

FELLOW TRAVELLER

Elaine S. Hochman. *Mies van der Rohe and the Third Reich.*
Weidenfeld & Nicolson, London 1989.

'Nazis, schmatzis', Philip Johnson observes on page 283 of this book, 'Mies would have built for anyone'. Alas this insight comes too late. History is more than hindsight, and the conduct of the butchers, bakers, candlestick makers (and architects) of Hitler's Germany still seems uniquely evil. The best that can be said of Elaine Hochman's perception of the life of Mies van der Rohe before he left Germany – in a book that is in the end more alarming in the promise of its swastika-decorated dust jacket and subtitle than in its massively footnoted text – is that she tries hard to swim against this tide. By work rather than talent (one of the architect's own aphorisms) she strives to understand the thoughts and actions of Mies van der Rohe as he moves – forwards not backwards – through the bewildering landscape of the first three decades of 20th century Germany. She traces his progress from pre-Great War camp-follower of the super-rich to private soldier; from post-Great War *proletkult* artist and manifesto-writer to Fascist fellow-traveller; from emigrant Green Card hunter to American architect but not, tantalizingly, to the inscrutable figure who returns after 30 years to raise a gaunt steel and glass art gallery in the flattened heart of West Berlin. Quite rightly she dwells on the lacunae that other biographers have glossed over. The Communist allegiances, the abandoned German wife and daughters, the 'Fighting League for German Culture', the 'Heil Hitler' letters, the 1934 Brussels Pavilion project, with its swastika and eagle. Quite wrongly she reconstructs out of quotations from a hundred historians and survivors of the period, paranoid interactions between Hitler and Mies that could never have occurred, simply because the architect was not then important enough for them to have mattered.

In the end all Hochman's efforts are fruitless. Though anecdotally rich her sustained curiosity about Nazism is always satisfied by assurances that Hitler was a psychopath – the personality type notorious throughout history for its ability to organize a 97 per cent vote of confidence at the drop of a hat. Nor will she accept unpalatable but interesting facts that somewhat vitiate the apparent prophetic skills of her characters, like the proven one that there was no German 'War Economy' until 1942.

Even at a personal level the motivations she attributes to Mies are diffuse and disproportionate. Thus at one point he is made to appear to want to leave for America because his Lange house project is refused planning permission. In fact he won a planning appeal and could have built it. A chapter or two later, he wants to leave because 'it is not unreasonable to assume' that he has heard of Hitler's 'monstrous (city planning) scheme that trampled over Berlin'. Then, only pages further on, it is suggested that he might have been offered the

Berlin plan commission himself! Finally the shortlisted architect for the Reichsbank ships out to design a summer cottage
in Wyoming for a director of the J. Walter Thompson advertising agency.

By the end of the book these false trails have become so
densely interwoven that the actions of the architect are at once
excused and rendered incomprehensible. Did he collaborate
with the Nazis? Did he run away? Or was he carried away by
the surprising number of Americans bearing half-job offers
that populate the later chapters? At various times Hochman
appears to say that either or both or all or one or none of these
is true, and as a result the book grinds itself into a kind of
argumentative rubble. The conclusion – that because we have
made it impossible for there ever again to be a Third Reich,
there can never again be a Mies van der Rohe – comes as
rather a surprise.

AGAINST THE 'GEOMETRIC ANIMAL'

Barbara Miller Lane. *Architecture and Politics in Germany*
1918–1945. Harvard University Press, Cambridge, MA 1968.

The New Man is no longer a man, he is a 'geometric animal'. He
needs no dwelling, no home, only a 'machine for living in'. This
man is not an individual, not a personality, but a collective entity,
a piece of mass man. And therefore they build 'housing develop-
ments', for him, apartment blocks of desolate uniformity, in
which everything is standardized.

Like a who dunnit cheater reading the last page first, this
reviewer sprang immediately to the pages covering the years
1933–1945 only to discover that it is Barbara Miller Lane's
thesis that the Nazi period derived its conception of aesthetic
and planning control as a political weapon from the activist
pioneers of the 1920s who, with different goals in mind, generated a polemical context in which discussions of art and

architecture were inseparable from heated debate about their social purpose. Nazi architecture, in effect, did not exist in isolation from the architecture of the Weimar Republic, it merely carried forward the 'debate' and, by means of legislative controls and harassment, 'discouraged' the more outspoken socialist Modernists.

Viewed in this light the Nazi identification of Bauhaus Modernism with *Kultur Bolschewismus* was not an irrational act of faith (as for instance was the blaming of the Jews for the worldwide Depression that began in 1929), but the logical outcome of 10 years of political infighting with the revolutionary politics of the Weimar Modernists.

This book is unilluminating as regards the ebb and flow of great reputations; eager Bauhaus skeleton-rattlers will be disappointed to see Hannes Meyer's tenure of office dismissed briefly and smoothly as 'politically turbulent'. Similarly disappointing is the book's lack of reference to the civil and military engineering manifestations of Nazi architecture which, although outside the strict terms of reference of the title, help to explain the apparently small amount of architectural work carried out between 1933 and 1945. In fact through her honest refusal to depict Nazi architecture as the mind bending means used by Adolf Hitler to reduce the German masses to servile obedience, the author lines up behind the historian A. J. P. Taylor, whose *Causes of the Second World War* depicts Hitler as a German statesman in the grand tradition of Bismarck and Stresemann, rather than as an evil genius. This interpretation, which might be termed the anticlimactic explanation of the Third Reich, explains otherwise confusing architectural evidence, such as the coexistence of the neo-Classic Zeppelinfeld in Nuremburg, the Olympic stadium in Berlin, the House of German Art in Munich, and other so-called 'Fuhrer buildings' including the *Ordensburgen* leadership schools, with the functional Luftwaffe headquarters and the folk-architecture Hitler Youth hostels and model villages built throughout Germany at the same time.

From this standpoint one is tempted to view the fate of the architecture of traumatic Germany as no more than a spectacular episode in the institutionalization of the architecture of the whole Western world. The development controls enforced by the Nazis after 1933 were scarcely less effective in restricting the growth of the new architecture of the Modern Movement than was the passage of the Town and Country Planning Acts in Britain 10 years later. The dehumanizing monumentality of the Zeppelinfeld is scarcely less dehumanizing than the Lincoln Memorial Center or any one of a dozen other major public structures erected in Europe and America since 1945.

These are murky waters to explore, but they will remain polluted until somebody explains why the quotation from the *Volkischer Beobachter* for February 1933 that opens this review is so astonishingly similar to the 1918 quotation from Henri Berlage which follows, or why both are so reminiscent of the press outcry over the partial collapse at Ronan Point that took place in 1968.

> The labourers see in the monotony which they fear in the rows upon rows of identical, bigger and smaller houses, an onslaught upon their individuality, their liberty, and their dignity as human beings. And now the housing development – once even drastically characterized in a revolutionary journal as 'one uniform, one food, one fold', suggests a cellular prison.

EXORCISING ADOLF

Michael Z. Wise. *Capital Dilemma: Germany's Search for a New Architecture of Democracy*. Princeton Architectural Press, Princeton, NJ 1998.

As this book powerfully reminds us, like bear-baiting the consumerization of architecture is a cruel sport that only the heartless can enjoy and only the resolute survive with dignity. During the 1980s English architecture went through an orgy of consumerization at the hands of a squad of witless young fogies egged on by a mischievous Prince. Birmingham City Library was described as 'a place for burning books'; competition-winning extension to the National Gallery became 'a fire station with a tower for the bell'; a Mies van der Rohe bank became 'a glass stump'; a microprocessor factory 'a modern version of a Victorian prison' and so on.

Of course this game did not originate in Britain. It famously flourished in Germany during the 1930s when National Socialist critics and politicians lammed into Bauhaus architecture with a similar vocabulary. The modern housing schemes that had been the pride of the Weimar Republic became 'collections of stationary sleeping cars' and 'cages for apes', 'aquariums' and 'stalls for horses'. Flat roofed buildings in general were held up to opprobrium because they were said to imply occupants with flat heads.

It might have been thought that the memory of that era of witless, non-technical, non-expert, threatening 'criticism' would have been sufficient to cure Germany of it for millennia, but apparently not. As *Capital Dilemma* makes abundantly clear, where architectural criticism is concerned the 1930s were but a dress rehearsal for the 1990s and the whole of Germany but a stand-in for the city of Berlin. With the reunification of the country and the decision to move the capital from Bonn to Berlin, a new era of demotic architectural criticism began that still smoulders like an Indonesian forest fire. Between 1991 and the present, funded by the US$12 billion allocated by the German government to the recapitalization of Berlin, the architectural profession and its baggage train of administrators, academics, critics and commentators has created a cross between a McCarthyite witch-hunt, a mass exorcism and a Marx Brothers film.

The witch-hunt is the search for 'Fascist elements' in all the designs for new Berlin buildings – not difficult to find when, as architect Hans Kollhoff complains, 'In this paranoid situation everything that has a stone facade and a large door is regarded as a fascist building'. The exorcism is the process of 'architecturally cleansing' former Nazi and Communist buildings so that they can safely be occupied by German government departments (the bizarre wrapping of the Reichstag by Christo being only one of many examples).

The Marx Brothers film is the parade of absurd opinions about the extent to which existing and projected Berlin buildings might betray the existence of new German plans for world domination. 'I am sure you have heard that Germany has been reunited', the author quotes Jay Leno, 'the only question now is when it will go on tour again'.

This last inflammatory idea is a leitmotif running through the whole book and, it must be said, one that is eagerly stoked by the author with unsubtle hints like 'We can occupy this building very easily', said senior finance ministry official Hans-Michael-Meyer-Sebastian as he sat in the aviation ministry where the bombings of Coventry, Rotterdam and Guernica were planned . . . .

Like these lapses into side-taking, Wise's journalistic background diminishes his stature but not his readability. His chapters stop and start and repeat themselves, betraying their origin in newspaper and magazine articles, but the saga he describes is so lunatic that this hardly matters. Like medieval divines his architects, critics, politicians and general purpose advisers spin a web of polemical ectoplasm so enormous that for long periods the reader forgets that it is the reconstruction of a city and a national government that the book is about and not a jury-squabble in a school of architecture. Not a single practical issue relating to planning, information technology, housing or transport is mentioned, and the only time energy consumption is discussed is in the context of the Foster and Partners Reichstag refurbishment, where it is explained that the architects 'took refuge in problem solving' as a way out of the 'debate' on whether they should be preserving Red Army graffiti or not. Who can blame them?

By the end of *Capital Dilemma*, excellent read though it is, one has grown heartily sick of the symbolism of the Reichsbank, the Reichstag, the Luftwaffe Building, the Ministry of Propaganda, countless modified competition schemes and the infinite bruisability of everyone concerned.

If what we read about here is as close as Berlin has got to the 'new architecture of democracy' of the book's subtitle, after spending over US$12 billion, it would surely have been better to stay in the one they made earlier in Bonn.

FOUR

Stars

Mies van der Rohe's Crown Hall, symbol of the crisis of Modernism, sinks into the sea. 1978 photomontage by Stanley Tigerman entitled 'The Sinking of the Titanic'. Source: ©Stanley Tigerman, Tigerman Fugman McCurry 1978.

Man has never been the same since God died.
He has taken it very hard. Why, you'd think it was only yesterday,
the way he takes it.
Not that he says much, but he laughs much louder than he used to,
And he can't bear to be left alone even for a minute,
and he can't
Sit still.

Edna St Vincent Millay 1936

UNTRAINED MASTER

David G. De Long. *Bruce Goff: Toward Absolute Architecture*. Architectural History Foundation and MIT Press, Cambridge, MA 1989.

Like a surprising number of immortal architects, Bruce Goff (1904–1982) had no formal academic training and started work on a drawing board at a very early age. By the time he was 14 one of his designs had been published and another was under construction. At the ripe old age of 21 he had designed 25 buildings and built 12 – a record that would not disgrace an architect twice his age. More importantly the buildings he did design and build became progressively more radical. Early influenced by Frank Lloyd Wright, who later took a proprietorial and not altogether beneficial interest in his career, Goff developed out of unpromising small town mid-American beginnings into a trumpeter of the romantic, expressionistic avant garde, securing the native American heartland against the inroads of the Bauhaus.

Born in Kansas, apprenticed in Oklahoma and settled for some years in Chicago, Goff developed a modest practice from a string of clever private houses. By 1940 his investigations into angled geometry for plans and sections had moved him far beyond the more conservative Wright. From 1947 to 1956 he taught at the University of Oklahoma at Norman and produced a string of idiosyncratic works of genius of which the spiral Bavinger house is the best known. He later went to live in Wright's Price tower in Bartlesville, only the second occupant to actually make use of the connected living and working apartments provided there.

De Long's study of Goff, the second he has written, is an exhaustive and objective work that is unlikely to be bettered for thoroughness and scholarship. He even finds room to explain Goff's notorious departure from Norman in disgrace.

A FRANCOPHILE AMERICAN

The Filter of Reason: The Work of Paul Nelson. Edited by Terence Riley and Joseph Abram. Rizzoli International, London 1990.

Just as our quality newspapers are locked in a life-and-death struggle of obituaries, desperately trying to glean from the daily fields of mortality one or two lives that can support a two-column picture and the recounting of some forgotten achievement, so are the curators of our museums and galleries perpetually looking out for what might be called necropolitan talent. For from the archives of the supporting cast of the great drama of Modernism come the exhibitions and books of the present.

The life of Paul Neslon (1895–1979) exemplifies the possibilities as well as the limitations of the genre. Forgotten by architectural history, he lay for years just below the surface of pre-war architecture and design mythology, along with Eileen Gray (recently exhumed), Bertram Goldberg, Gilmer Black, George Fred Keck, Starling Burgess and many others.

Now, in this elegantly produced but scanty museum catalogue, he is so outrageously puffed up that at one point in the book we are told he 'elaborated the technological vision of Buckminster Fuller'. In fact Nelson steadfastly remains a small-calibre man. Despite the best that Terence Riley and Joseph Abram can do to dramatize his writings and his correspondence with the great and good, the Francophile American who divided his life between Europe and the US remains best known for the sets he designed for an unsuccessful 1929 Gloria Swanson film called 'What a Widow!' and the monster American Memorial Hospital he built in France in 1946 to expiate the destruction of the town of Saint-Lo during the war. His only innovative works were the ungainly metal Suspended House project of 1936 – consisting of a model and drawing of a dwelling which no amount of sympathetic redrawing and model making today can make look more appetizing than a dismal exercise in Deconstructivist bricolage – and its successor the 1938 Palace of Discovery.

The house design consisted only of a crude model with, allegedly, a Buckminster Fuller bathroom unit inside it. But despite this weakness it is elevated by Riley and Abram to something like the revolutionary status of Le Corbusier's Maison Domino.

The source of inspiration for the Palace of Discovery, which was Nelson's project for a monster, mast-supported exhibition hall, is assumed by his editors to be Buckminster Fuller, with whom Nelson corresponded for many years. But from its appearance it looks as though it was more likely derived from Le Corbusier's tension-braced Pavillion des Temps Nouveau of 1937 or even his much older Palace of the Soviets competition entry. Indeed the unacknowledged influence of Le Corbusier seems to pervade the work, not only of Nelson, but of his inspirers too. Riley even suggests in one footnote that Buckminster Fuller copied his 1927 4-D manuscript from *Vers une Architecture.*

Apart from occasionally intriguing matters of this kind the book contains a number of small reproductions of Nelson's unimpressive Miroesque paintings and snippets from his writings.

ONCE THERE WAS A RICH MAN

Cities of Artificial Excavation: The Work of Peter Eisenman 1978–1988. Edited by Jean-Francois Bedard. Canadian Centre for Architecture/Rizzoli International Publications, New York 1995.

Once upon a time Peter Eisenman was real enough to have had his American Express card revoked – or so he said. But it was many years ago, when his New York Institute of Architecture and Urban Studies was run on a shoestring, before he became the subject of his own and others' deep investigations. Before, in fact, he became both guru and gauleiter, artist and American ambassador at large. Now a great bear of a man growling, 'Shear, Shear!' to his staff as they whittle away at foamboard models and bring in sandwiches for dinner and breakfast, as well as lunch, the Eisenman of the smile and shoeshine days was somehow different. Not that he made much more sense but, like Alvin Boyarsky, he was different.

Somewhere along the line something terrible must have happened to him to bring him under the Canadian microscope of Jean-Francois Bedard. Too late now to pretend that the famous 'Ten Houses' were a mistake, or a joke. Now they are deadly serious, examined with the forensic skill of a hunter studying spores. 'Cities of Artificial Excavation' was published to coincide with an exhibition of the same name at the Canadian Centre for Architecture last year. It contains numerous essays of commentary upon Eisenman and his work, including a contribution to the general muddying of the waters by Eisenman himself. There is not much that is critical in this book. Eisenman and his work during the decade 1978–1988 are subjected to a very detailed treatment but the net result is praise, if not self-praise. And if not self-praise then confusion, for the volume abounds in graphic non-sequiturs that make following it from beginning to end a mug's game. Among the essays probably the least unreadable is that of Alan Balfour, new head of school at Rensselaer Polytechnic Institute, late of the AA in London. Others by Kurt Forster, Jean Louis Cohen, Frederic Jameson and Bedard himself enjoy only occasional periods of lucidity.

FORCE OF PERSONALITY

Mats Egelius. *Ralph Erskine, Architect*. Byggforlaget in conjunction with the Swedish Museum of Architecture, Stockholm 1991.

There is a photograph on page 151 of this excellent book that tells the entire truth about Ralph Erskine. It is an unusual aerial view of the Byker estate in Newcastle showing the mighty sinuous 'wall' sheltering its clusters of two-storey houses. From the air the planting and landscaping diminish in importance and whole project looks far less attractive than it does at ground level. In fact it looks Anglo-Corbusian, like an extension of one of those two notorious examples of 1960s 'utopian' public housing, Parkhill and Hyde Park.

Yet while the Sheffield estates are a byword for dehumanized Modernism, with their high level walkways and 'streets in the air', Byker has gone down in history as a pioneering piece of 'community architecture' where the wishes of the occupants guided the designer's pencil. How can this be?

The answer is that Erskine gets his way. In an astonishing career spanning 50 years he has never failed to write his signature on every project he has designed; from the tiny one-roomed house he and his wife built for themselves in Sweden in 1941, through the projects of the 1950s that brought him to international attention, down to the ticky-tackiest tract housing for Milton Keynes that he designed in the 1970s, up to Clare College and Byker and now the spectacular tri-coloured 22-storey Lilla Bommen office block in Goteborg, and the London Ark itself.

At the age of 77, Erskine can look back on a life of conviction. He has always been able to convince his clients that they are right to pay for what was, and still is, a breathtakingly amateur kind of pre-war Modernism.

Erskine has never been a programmatic architect, dedicated to finding God in the details, rather he has seen God in the outline and let the craftsman fill in the details for him.

Ralph Erskine, as Mats Egelius perceptively notes, took from his Quaker origins the habit of speaking openly to everyone and to no one in particular. A friendly and agreeable man, he never oversteps the limits of agreeableness. Like any successful salesman, who will never intensify his relationship with a customer beyond the matter of selling, Erskine will, nonetheless wear down his subject with agreeableness until he or she gives in and buys what he is selling.

That he does this by force of personality rather than argument is indisputable. For where Erskine does advance theories about architecture they are, as Egelius again perceptively notes, simple to the point of naivety. Shelter, hearth, land, sun and wind is all there is to it. Not a touch of urban sophistication, not a breath of post-Modern symbolism. Yet in his work there is always the presence of deeply enigmatic shapes that hint at deeper meanings.

Ralph Erskine has never ceased to be what he proudly calls 'a primitive functionalist', and has never abandoned the principles of Socialism and the Modern Movement as he understood both in the 1930s. A student at that time he declaimed

Left-Wing politics from his drawing board at the Regent Street Polytechnic in London and strongly supported the Republican side in the Spanish Civil War. How he has reconciled these early beliefs with the bewildering changes that have overtaken him since is a theme that Egelius explores with more tenacity than any previous critic or biographer. As a result it is unlikely that there will be another book in this awe-inspiring figure's lifetime that is as sympathetic, authoritative and yet also satisfyingly inquiring.

DEATH OF AN ENGINEER

Peter Rice. *An Engineer Imagines*. Artemis, London 1994.

The deaths of great engineers exert a powerful fascination. On May 2nd 1859 Isambard Kingdom Brunel, very near to death, was drawn in an open wagon across the Royal Albert Bridge at Saltash, linking the counties of Devon and Cornwall. Almost complete, the great suspension bridge which survives to this day, its loads counteracted by huge curved wrought iron tubes, was his railway masterpiece, and one of the last sights he ever saw.

For the great engineer Peter Rice the end was different. He died on October 25th 1992 at the age of 57 from the effects of a brain tumour diagnosed in the previous year. Unlike Brunel – who died even younger at 53 and brought on the stroke that killed him by overwork – Rice had time to become reconciled to his approaching end. Some 6 months before, he wrote a poem about it in which he summarized the advantages of an early death: 'To die, not old, coccooned in love/Transferring through a point in time/To somewhere else/A gift we have no right to ask/And it is mine'.

The name of Peter Rice is not as well known today as were the names of the great 19th century structural engineers. Yet Rice worked on projects that are not so much household names as household images in our own time. Born in Dundalk in 1935, son of the education officer for County Louth, he was destined for the priesthood but chose engineering instead. Graduating from Queen's University, Belfast, he came to London in 1956 to do graduate work and took a job with Ove Arup and Partners, consulting engineers. Advanced rapidly by his mentor, the leader of the firm Sir Ove Arup, the only other engineer recipient of the Royal Gold Medal for Architecture that Rice was eventually to receive himself and a man Rice described as 'my father in engineering', he started out as a junior engineer on the project to build the virtually unbuildable Sydney Opera House, designed by the Danish architect Bjorn Utzon. Ten years later, with the Opera House behind him, he moved to Paris to design the structure for the Centre Pompidou for two more competition winners, the architects Renzo Piano and Richard Rogers. After the completion of Pompidou in 1976 he worked with Piano on other projects, including the Menil Museum in Texas, the monster Kansai International Airport in Japan and the ocean liner *Crown Princess*. He worked with Rogers again too, most notably on the Lloyd's building. His was the engineering skill that structured the glass pyramid at the Louvre for I. M. Pei, the fabric sail of the Grande Arche at La Defense and the extraordinarily attenuated stone arches of the Pavilion of the Future at the Seville Expo of 1992. In the last years of his life he worked on an astonishing number and variety of projects, all listed in an appendix to the book. They ranged from a new car for FIAT and structuring a tent for the Museum of the Moving Image for Future Systems, to designing a mountain for EuroDisney. Rice did calculations for yachts, bridges, buildings and fabric structures without end. As Renzo Piano once remarked, he could design structures 'like a pianist who can play with his eyes shut'.

As Rice's reputation grew, any architect, anywhere in the world, who won a significant competition, invariably sought his help. The news that Peter Rice was on the team stilled all anxiety about a project's feasibility. At the height of the 1980s building boom such calls for help were coming at the rate of a dozen a day. If, as Brunel once sardonically observed, the term 'consulting engineer' meant no more than 'a man who, for a consideration, sells his name and nothing more', then

Rice virtually gave his name away. Yet he did so not solely on the strength of a palette of modern materials and methods so far beyond the wildest dreams of any Victorian engineer as to make everything easy. He radiated a tremendous personal confidence as well and that confidence was also for hire.

Underlying Rice's modesty, which he maintained throughout his life, despite his immense professional, if not public reputation, was a continued insistence that, however crucial his role as an engineer might be, it was the architect's task to determine the visual importance of the different elements in any building structure and thus determine its appearance. By insisting upon this division of powers from the outset, Rice always allowed the architects who consulted him to retain the dominant vision in the design process. This was a completely altruistic motivation, for he never betrayed ill will towards those who became world famous as a result of his efforts. It might have been Peter Rice who made the Centre Pompidou work, with his vast cast steel *gerberettes*, but it was Renzo Piano and Richard Rogers who determined *how it would look*, and thus in the public mind they remain its creators.

In this autobiographical volume, which abounds in random insights but inevitably, having been started too late, is not a structured narrative, the reader can see how Rice's self-effacing style kept him aloof from style wars and ideological issues. 'Information never interested me', he wrote. 'I can't read and absorb it. I always learn the minimum necessary. It is still the way'. His minimalism was expressed in other ways too. A man who worked on advanced structures all over the world, he lived modestly with his family in Shepherds Bush and drove a battered Citroen so as not to attract attention. He took no position on the North/South conflict between the austere constructivist engineering tradition of the Anglo-Saxons and the challenging Hispanic approach with its sensually curved structures. In the same way his amenability to the frivolities of post-Modern and Conceptual architecture exasperated some and attested to a playfulness, perhaps in the end a kind of nihilism about all style and ideology in design.

Apart from an alert opening chapter about the Pompidou project, and an absorbing reflection on his childhood in

Ireland, the cleverest and shortest chapter in the book is one devoted to architectural photography, and the growing effect it is having upon the design of buildings. And the cleverest image is of a slice of translucent stone framed in opaque stone from the new West front of Lille Cathedral. A paradox of the kind that pleased him.

'MUM, I'VE WON BEAUBOURG!'

Bryan Appleyard. *Richard Rogers: A Biography.*
Faber & Faber, London 1986.

There are books about architecture that make their author famous and there are books about architects that make their subject famous. In the last 15 years the former have so grossly outweighed the latter that the whole genre has become distorted into a branch of art history with staging posts all over the lush pastures of American academe. Books about architects that actually tell us anything about the lives of these fugitives, whose survival as an independent species is more drastically threatened than that of the osprey or the Bengal tiger, are thinner on the ground than suits from Nic's Toggery in Tallahassee. You can in fact draw a line from Esther McCoy's *Five California Architects* published in 1960 to *Richard Rogers: A Biography* published more than a quarter of a century later and not strike a single example in between – that is how good a book Bryan Appleyard has written.

Rogers is joint architect of the Centre Beaubourg in Paris, allegedly the most visited public building of the second half of the 20th century, and sole architect of the new Lloyd's building in the City of London. Both were won in competition and both are uncompromisingly high-tech buildings heavily dependent on structural and service engineering, de-culturalized in the modern manner so that 'meaning' in the art historical sense is applied to them rather than being indigenous: something that arrives electronically, rather than being whipped up out of anachronistic ornament. There are more extreme examples of this, to be sure, but not more character-istic ones. If there were a time capsule big enough to hold the aspirations of the last generation of architects to be taught Modernism without guilt, one or other would arguably be the best choice to go into it. Rogers' buildings embody all that is best and worst about high-technology building design: they stand clearly at the crisis point of today – when society is deciding whether to allow architecture to go ahead as a branch of technology, like aerospace or computers, or force it to revert to an historical vocabulary, hiding the electronic wiz-ardry of the future behind phony historical facades. It is very important to know about the people who want to make the first choice so that we can measure them against the conser-vationists and the classical revivalists who want to make the second; doubly important because the historical crowd have so far made such a splendid job of depicting themselves as straightforward, decent men and women who are as mad as hell and not going to take modern architecture any more.

Appleyard presents Rogers as a kind of ageing hippie. A survivor of the early years of rock and roll who contrived, like the younger (but not much) Paul McCartney and Mick Jagger, to age intelligibly enough to provide a principled, non-suicidal role model for those who follow. This too is a major bio-graphical achievement, however common it might be in the world of show business, music, sport or even space travel. Indeed at his best Appleyard achieves something of the warmth and clarity of Tom Wolfe in *The Right Stuff*, explain-ing the life of a technological man in terms that are neither naive nor post-heroic. Richard Rogers has his ups and downs, from prep school to late middle age. When he is hurt and rejected, he bleeds and suffers: when he is loved and wins great commissions, he has a slap-up feed and gives jobs to all his friends. Like the great figures of rock and roll he puts life, love, babies, business, and money together into a great big pot and makes that into his career. There is no public man and private man, only Richard Rogers, *sans complexe*.

This achievement, both existential and biographical, cannot really be dismissed as 'showbiz' or 'Dynasty', as some art his-torical architectural critics have done. Rogers is a success in a profession most of whose members barely earn enough to apply for an American Express card, let alone manage to express creative ideas in their work. Architects today are hovering on the brink of ephemeralization – about to vanish into the humourless button-down world of the construction industry without a trace. One model of a man who did it his way is of incalculable value to their morale. Appleyard's life of Rogers will actually make younger readers want to be architects when they grow up – again no small achievement in a profession committed to cutting the number of its own students by one-third in order to safeguard the tenuous livelihood of the remainder.

The book is not perfect, but even its weaknesses help it in the end. For every blissful passage full of youth, carelessness, vagabondage and comedy, there is a desperate page or two trying to sum up the architectural *zeitgeist* in respectable academic terms. Luckily Appleyard is not very good at this and he soon flips back to riveting, gossipy phenomenology. For this he is apparently being blamed by some members of the extended Rogers family. A pity, for what he has done is a wonderful act of liberation.

BEST TOUR SINCE ROLLING THUNDER

Richard Rogers + Architects. Architectural Monographs Series edited by Frank Russell. Academy Editions, London 1986.

Looking at the painfully straight laced 'good-guy' pages of *Richard Rogers + Architects* after reading Bryan Appleyard is a sobering experience. Here are pictures of Rogers' early houses at Murray Mews where the builder used black-painted paper instead of a proper damp proof course. No mention of that in Frank Russell's pages. The plants at Creek Vean that all died? Nothing about that either. The endless pages of wonderfully cool, depersonalized technical drawing here makes you realize how much humanity has been booted out of the typical architectural practice book – and at what cost in sheer existential excitement. The origin of the bizarre notion of the architect's 'arrogance', is precisely this timid, ascetic, error-free, genius guaranteed gang of do-gooders and their works that Russell presents. Only the best writers on architecture, Ayn Rand, Esther McCoy, Tom Wolfe, know that it is not and never was like that.

With any luck a combination of Appleyard's blood transfusion and Academy Editions painstaking detail might become the norm for other architectural biographies in the future. Provided today's young practitioners do not neglect their swashbuckling of course.

THE ACCEPTABLE FACE OF HIGH-TECH

Deyan Sudjic. *The Architecture of Richard Rogers*. 4th Estate, London 1994.

Unlike most famous architects, Richard Rogers is not an inaccessible man. Or so it at first appears. From time to time he dines in his wife's famous restaurant in full view of the other patrons and is generally well disposed towards the media. A telephone call from a magazine requesting an interview will be fielded with the cheerful offer of an hour in the architect's 'next media window', some 2 or 3 months ahead. The request will then be 'pencilled in' for that time. When the time finally arrives, the interview will be postponed or take place implausibly late, but that is not rudeness, it is life. Rogers is genuinely obliging. The persistent journalist, like the patient gunner, will always get his man in the end.

When the interviewer does encounter the charismatic figure, another kind of problem arises. Rogers is a genial though indistinct speaker and woe betide the interrogator who relies on a tape recorder. The man who half-created Pompidou and did create Lloyds – the two best known edifices of late 20th century architecture in Europe – is notorious for his streaming consciousness and eliding diction. Here is genius, the visitor is sure. But how to find it out? This is the problem faced on a larger scale by all Rogers biographers, and only the non-architect Brian Appleyard has ever successfully solved it.

Deyan Sudjic knows Rogers well. He has written about him and his work for years. Not scandalously, like Appleyard, perhaps, but perceptively, and not always with slavish devotion. The difference between the two biographers is that Appleyard expressed fascination with the events of Rogers' surprising life, while Sudjic is more impressed by the translation from architect to personality to political figure that has taken place in his subject over the last decade. The Richard Rogers brought to prominence as one of the triumvirs in the celebrated Royal Academy Exhibition Foster, Rogers, Stirling in 1986, is now more clearly seen as a figure on his own. Stirling is dead, Foster has become a world figure, with offices in Asia as well as Battersea, and only Rogers remains, though also capable of global operations, still a local force, devoted to London's good causes, a trustee of this, a patron of that, an advisor on architecture and planning to the Labour Party. A man poised in fact to become the paterfamilias of all of architecture in Britain with the next change of government. And this in the end may be his epitaph. He understood in that troubled and disempirialized offshore island that such a position was open to a great architect. As Sudjic writes; 'Most architects are too inept or unworldly to understand the elementary rules of social conduct which allow them to take on such roles'.

Although well illustrated and readable – except of course for its tiny-type/big-pic graphic design – the text of *The Architecture of Richard Rogers* bears the imprint of summary objectivity if not haste. The anticipated insider dealing Sudjic insights are present, but sparingly used. In the end it is the absence of Rogers the person, pointed up by a revealing dearth of direct quotations, that says it all. The next media window may not be for some time to come.

ALL RIOT ON THE WESTERN FRONT

Charles Jencks. *Heteropolis: Los Angeles, the Riots and the Strange Beauty of Hetero-Architecture*. Academy Group, London 1993.

It is difficult to imagine the horror and beauty of Los Angeles, except perhaps at moments during the Notting Hill Carnival when you wonder idly what all this would be like with the addition of an overhead freeway system and an earthquake. In Los Angeles there are helicopters in the sky day and night, the Eastern horizon is yellow with pollution, the traffic on the packed freeways can stand still as a photograph and all around you TV policemen stare through dark glasses like prison officers waiting for the mother of all riots to begin. Besides that, there is some wacky architecture there.

If its wacky Los Angeles architecture you are interested in, this is your book. Right smack on the cover is a wacky building fronted by a giant pair of binoculars. Inside is a frenzied text by Dr Charles Jencks, the world's leading expatriate Anglophile American architectural theorist and historian, the Godfather of post-Modern architecture, and a man who puts his money where his mouth is by decamping for part of every year from Holland Park to Santa Monica.

Compared to the late Reyner Banham, who rode a bicycle and wrote in a blithely uncomprehending fashion about all the threatening cross-currents of Angelino life, Jencks is marinated in social realism. He starts off with the 1992 Rodney King riots in his subtitle and, inside the book, sparks up the usual Los Angeles parade of cheap and cheerful 'designer' restaurants, diners, bars, shops and 'art buildings', with coloured maps that explain the ethnic make-up of the city and show where the riots were. His text oscillates wildly from neologisms – 'Heteropolis' (a city of differences), 'Cosmopolis' (a city of tourists and visitors), 'En-formality' (environmental formalism) – to impenetrable lists of allegedly creative persons which no reviewer could ever do justice to. Everywhere, in his mission to explain the megalopolis of Los Angeles, Jencks sinks up to his axles in what Banham used warily to call 'heavy stuff'. He shows many pictures of buildings, but also pictures of blazing neighbourhoods and strife-torn supermarkets. There are mentions of the 'browning of America' and allusions to the coming world where 'heterosexual male confronts female and gay'. DNA comes into Jencks's narrative, and so do unburned hydrocarbons, the environment, *Blade*

Runner and finally something called 'heteropolitanbioregion-alism'. Luckily, as he reminds us at the very beginning of the book, 'the main problem facing us today is the destruction of the ecosphere and the mass-extinction of species'. If it were not, clearly we might have a lot more to understand.

Appropriately enough, the original title of this book was 'A Walk through the Post-Modern Pluriverse'. Jencks intended it to be at least 400 pages long, dealing with the whole cultural phenomenon of post-Modernism in the world. Then, last Spring, the riots happened and, like the bounty hunter he is, Jencks saw his opportunity. His walk through the post-Modern universe became a run through South central Los Angeles.

'Only Connect!', he cried and, grabbing the zapping power cable of interracial conflict, jammed it into the dead socket of ticky-tacky Los Angeles pomo and Wow! The flash lit up the heavens. Miraculously Los Angeles architecture came back to life. Money poured into riot-stricken areas. Guilty policemen were punished and *Heteropolis* was published.

The key figure in Jencks' link between architecture and riot is Los Angeles architect Frank Gehry. Toronto born, Gehry is a freewheeling 60-something architectural genius Jencks particularly admires, so much so that in *Heteropolis* he has constructed a kind of genealogical table showing how he is descended from Charles Eames, Rudolf Schindler, Jane Jacobs and Walt Disney. More than that, Gehry is the one Los Angeles architect with a world reputation who really did respond to the Rodney King riots. Deeply into such tiresome creative games as fixing real aeroplanes to the sides of buildings and designing others so they looked like fish, he took the comprehensive burning down of previously non-violent neighbourhoods very hard. When he learned that the rioters had looted gun stores, Gehry had a biblical vision of the four policemen of the apocalypse galloping down the freeway. He offered places in his office to youngsters from the riot district and embarked on local area redevelopment programmes.

'You hope they are going to need architecture', says Gehry about this whole business, 'but they don't. They are culturally very rich. They don't need architecture, they need self-respect'.

Jencks is quick on his feet. By the end of *Heteropolis* he is pinning his faith on the way that plants from all over the world have been able to grow and flourish in California. Perhaps, he wonders, after this headlong but strangely optimistic tour of tinderbox tinseltown, all the people there from all over the world might learn to do the same thing.

TALE OF A GREAT INFLUENCE

Edited by Richard Economakis. *Leon Krier: Architecture and Urban Design.* Academy Editions, London 1993.

In an age of political correctness, crowded with public figures desperate not to attract attention to themselves, and determined always to keep open a line of retreat, Leon Krier used to be a daring exception. Born in Luxembourg in 1946, the son of an ecclesiastical tailor, he grew to maturity in the 1960s at the height of the Modern Movement in architecture and design. But as a student at the Technical University of Stuttgart, Krier spurned Modern orthodoxy. He also elected to play no part in the revolt of the young. When academic disturbances broke out all over Europe in the wake of the Events of May 1968, he attended a conference on the colonization of outer space. In fact, so unorthodox was his training that, despite his tremendous reputation in architecture and planning today, he spent only 1 year as a student, during which he presented classical designs to his bemused Modernist professors and they in turn awarded him no grades. At the end of it all he came to London to work for the late Sir James Stirling.

Krier loathed London – 'Luxembourg City with a population of 60 000 is more urban than London', he once said – but his visit proved fruitful. Stirling was then in the cusp of his shocking abandonment of Modernism in favour of an extravagant post-Modern Classicism of his own devising, while Krier was sorely in need of a more convincing drafting style. Krier's ideological strength may have helped his new mentor to step decisively into the post-Modern camp, but Stirling's facility at drawing certainly flowed into Krier's veins like plasma. From that point onwards he produced city plans, entered architectural competitions, and proselytized for a Classical revival in architecture without rest or restraint.

By the mid-1970s Krier was so far outside the mainstream of architectural thought that he flirted with the architectural equivalent of excommunication by befriending the late Albert Speer, Hitler's architect and a convicted war criminal. Krier then published the definitive volume on Speer's work – virtually all of it destroyed in World War Two. In the following decade he continued to *epater le bourgeois*. In 1983, in a celebrated article published in *Die Welt*, he claimed that Hitler's rocket man (and later NASA Apollo spacecraft designer) Werner von Braun should have been imprisoned in Spandau, while Speer should have been taken to America to replan Washington, DC. In the same article he argued that the Modern city of Milton Keynes and the concentration camps at Auschwitz and Birkenau were 'children of the same parents'. More recently he has suggested, so great does he believe the destructive force of Modernism to have been, that a whole generation has now grown up with no understanding of beauty because of it. 'They consider a classical column more dangerous than a nuclear power station', he said in a recent lecture, 'and fear pornography because they do not understand that it is beautiful'.

How this unlikely figure of the early 1980s, with his wild hair and rusting Peugeot car, displaying all the disregard for money or critical acclaim of a true artist, ever came to plan vacation communities in Florida, masterplan the Prince of Wales's forthcoming Potemkin village at Dorchester and not only become our future monarch's leading architectural adviser but, through him, become a guru to the rulers of all Europe's ancient cities, is difficult to understand. This family bible-sized volume on his work, with 'over 2000 drawings', does not explain it, any more than Krier does himself, in the extremely short introduction in which he draws a sardonic parallel between the '45 000 Allied bullets' it took 'to kill one German soldier in World War Two' and the '10 000 architectural drawings' he has made over the last 25 years leading only to the building of 'a small house, three podiums for sculptures and planning permission for a small town'.

Krier's '10 000 architectural drawings', with their thin pencil lines, axial geometry and whimsically overflying biplanes – the once frequent zeppelins seem to have been censored out – express ideas about urbanism that are elementary, but dangerously seductive. His 1988 scheme for 'Atlantis, a new town in Tenerife', for example, is drawn directly from the Babylonian subconscious of Cecil B. de Mille, with no evidence of modern life present in its ravishingly rendered street scenes, except an occasional figure in modern dress. And this is the heart of his method. His cities solve Modern problems by banishing them. There are no motorway networks, no public transport systems, no electronic communications, no street signs and the only movement is by bicycle or on foot. From Spitalfields to Washington, DC his recipe is always the same: multi-centric, multi-functional urban space to obviate commuting; immense new public buildings, pyramids, towers, monuments, churches and temples (all Classical, Gothic or post-Modern in appearance); the banishment of motor cars (except for here and there a picturesque example); the extravagant use of great areas of water and a vast indulgence in great flights of steps. Professional and lay-person alike, gazing at the projects in this beautifully laid out and printed book must be both attracted and repelled. The picture of Krier it portrays is at once prolific, cynical, clever, nostalgic and carefully selected for the 1990s. There is, for instance, no reference to his interesting thoughts on Albert Speer, Auschwitz, Milton Keynes or pornography in it anywhere at all.

WRAPPING THE REICHSTAG

Christo: The Reichstag and Urban Projects.
Edited by Jacob Baal-Teshuva. Prestel, London 1994.

When last February, to the rage of Chancellor Helmut Kohl, and the joy of Speaker Rita Sussmuth, the German parliament voted to authorize the wrapping of the Berlin Reichstag by the Bulgarian artist Christo, an era of German history came to an end. The question is, did an era in art history end too. There is, after all, a sameness about Christo's wrapping projects that is enhanced by their extensive prevision in drawings, photomontages and books like this one. Seen in these pages the Monument to Victor Emanuel in Milan, the Pont Neuf in Paris and, yes, even like the wrapped footpaths in Kansas City, all share this ho-hum quality. Christo has done other things too, of course, but his high-profile project to pass the parcel in Berlin is not one of them. Even the details about recycling the vast quantity of PVC-reinforced fabric to the Third World and fitting special cages to protect 'delicate protuberances' fail to lift the narrative above the gloomy suspicion that wrapping up the Reichstag is just another kind of graffiti on a historic building, after which the old place can never be the same.

As though to head the charge of mercenary opportunism off at the pass, Christo's editor makes much of the fact that the project began in 1971, when there was still a Berlin Wall, and has since undergone an ordeal of permissions, approvals and changes of mind matching those of the British Library. This may be so, but now the project is scheduled to be executed in 1995, when there is one Germany that is a very different place and an architectural solution to the rehabilitation of the building that can only get in the way.

Despite its world reputation, the Berlin Reichstag was the seat of government in Germany for only 10 of the 100 years that have passed since its completion. Ever since 1894 the Reichstag, the creation of an otherwise unknown Frankfurt architect named Paul Wallot, has enjoyed a history dogged by misfortune. Now last year's competition for the transformation of the building, from which Sir Norman Foster and Partners emerged triumphant, threatens to collide with Christo's unique solution to all architectural swamps of lost opportunities. Not that any of this is Sir Norman Foster's fault, any more than it is Christo's. Nonetheless it does seem that the building is cursed, and that nothing will ever change its historic role as a grim reminder of the rise of Nazism and the terror bombing of Germany – not even the timely pre-production of this jolly book, ready last year, and now probably destined to go on selling till the end of the century.

ONE MAN MESSIAH

Victor Papanek. *Design for the Real World*, 2nd edition, completely revised. Academy Chicago Publishers, Chicago 1986.

Victor Papanek. *Design for Human Scale*. Van Nostrand Reinhold, New York 1986.

'When you try to tell people in the West that within a very short time millions may die of hunger, they simply do not hear. They give a little nervous laugh; embarrassed, they change the subject.' Especially, this reviewer is tempted to add, if they are in a restaurant.

The trouble with Victor Papanek is that he is drowning in self-praise while the rest of the world gives a little nervous laugh. Wherever he writes and lectures he is introduced as a prodigy, a polymath who has worked – no, 'Lived and taught' – in 14 countries; as the author of the most widely read design book of all time; as the inventor of 'Biomorphic Design' (wasn't that Richard Neutra?); as a consultant to almost every international body of any significance you have ever heard of; as a Nobel Prizewinner – no, I misread that, as an ALTERNATIVE Nobel Prize NOMINEE and as a distinguished professor of architecture. Is there more? Probably, but there is only so much room on a book jacket. Is he responsible for his own publisher's blurbs? Well, yes, because their tone is actually drawn from his own dense and hortatory texts, rather than packaged around them, with the result that puff and exaggeration have become in the end indistinguishable from the man himself. When, for instance, on page 146 of the revised edition of *Design for the Real World* he reports having received an apparently sympathetic letter from Alastair Best, editor of *Designer* magazine in London – a modest publication circulated to members of the Society of Industrial

Artists and Designers – Best becomes 'Editor-in-Chief' and his magazine 'the most influential magazine on design in the world'. What is the difference between this unnecessary piece of self importance and the quote from a review by 'Sir Anthony Wedgwood Benn' (a man who does not exist) that adorns the back cover of *Design for the Real World*? Perhaps the answer lies in the curious information supplied on page 171 that, unlike many thinkers, Papanek works best against a background of 'Phones ringing, frequent interruptions, and a great deal of visual distraction'.

Like Ralph Nader, Papanek has made a career, not so much out of ideas as out of dubiously authoritative information, but his career has lasted longer, and the longer it lasts the more names he is able to drag into it. The bibliography in the first edition of *Design for the Real World* ran to 500 entries – the presence of few of which were adequately explained by any connection with the author's own work – this second edition boasts a bibliography almost twice as long, but there is a catch. The reader is cautioned that the only two books published since the first edition that really match up to the author's exacting standards have not yet been translated into English. Does Papanek mind this splendid isolation? Well no, one suspects he does not. In the world of design education – if not design itself – he is famous as the man who can spot un-ecological gewgaws from 5 miles away and always spell the manufacturer's name right.

Papanek is the design writer so proud of having said in 1971 that industrial designers 'like killing people' that he repeats the charge verbatim. Papanek is the man who saw that the design of the Kodak Carousel slide projector was getting worse instead of better. And Papanek, as popular mythology has it, is the man who revolutionized car production at Volvo by getting away from the production line . . . Just before the line was painlessly taken over by robots.

The trouble with *Design for the Real World* and *Design for Human Scale*, which claims to deal in more detail with the same subject, the misfit of design and 'human needs', is that they are both 51 per cent right. Each book consists of a vast bundle of indictments larded with brand names, and a slightly smaller number of brisk outlines of how things might be done differently and better. When Papanek says that all industrial design should be derived from total planetary energy economics, he is entirely correct; as of course he is when he draws attention, however ineffectively, to the spectre of famine. But alas, the Walkmen and Star Wars video games that he excoriates not only outnumber his own tin-can radios in the unrecognizable place he calls 'The Third World', but are preferred by the citizens of those very societies he maintains can teach us all about ecologically responsible design. If 'The Third World' is failing to teach us old tricks, Papanek sees their failure as the result of a global conspiracy of the 'Northern' nations to put all the wrong things their way – a thesis he advances with such vigour that one cannot help wondering about his own encounters with the chauffeur-driven Mercedes-riding politicians of Africa. Does he use one of his own pedal-driven trucks to get to those vital meetings at the ministry?

Quite apart from embodying in his own life of consultancy many of the contradictions he so exasperatingly discerns in others, Papanek is just as often wrong in his own problem analysis. His case for the return of the sailing ship is a good example. Made in the first edition of *Design for the Real World* and claimed to have been vindicated in the second by recent experiments, it has not only been put on the back burner once more by collapsing oil prices but was misconceived in the first place. Sailing ships did not become obsolete because of their lack of speed or because of the large number of men necessary to operate their sails. As long ago as 1904 the schooner *Thomas W. Lawson* of 4000 tons boasted steam powered running rigging and a crew of just seven; her speed in a trade wind was far above the cruising speed of a supertanker. Any yachtsman could have told Papanek that the real reason for the demise of the clipper ship was the quantum leap in passage-keeping reliability that was the immediate benefit of steam, and the construction of the Suez and Panama canals. Even if satellite navigation and computer controlled sails could somewhat even the balance today, fuel cost is less important than movement programming where shipping logistics are concerned and no modern commercial sailing ship would ever be allowed to put to sea without auxiliary engines, so the savings would be marginal. Under these circumstances it is difficult to see how the return of the sailing ship is a 'solution' to anything except the problem of leisure that Papanek affects to despise, so the big simple argument is down to 1 per cent.

Papanek may know this, just as he may be familiar with the same sort of arguments that hinder the return of the dirigible; the Third World triumph of the pedal-powered truck; the replacement of the 'huge steel coffin' of the automobile by the $995 electrically powered aluminium scooter; the beneficial use of roller skates in factories and distribution centres and so on. And if he knows that, he also knows that, while such superficially obvious solutions are greeted rapturously by students of architecture and design, the real world, so far from being designed, slips more and more certainly out of control.

0% CREDIT

OMA, Rem Koolhaas and Bruce Mau. *S,M,L,XL.*
Uitgeverij 010, Rotterdam 1997.

There has not been a book as heavy as Rem Koolhaas's magnum opus since libraries stopped lending the complete works of Jeffrey Archer, yet despite its old-fashioned bigness, it is a book that no architectural reviewer has been able to understand. Instead of straightforwardly describing it as the final solution to the narrative problem (which in literary terms is what it is) all of them have searched instead for the key to post-post-Modernism somewhere in its pages – the very thing that does not exist. Despite what it says on the jacket, *S,M,L,XL* is not a novel about architecture. Despite New York *Vogue*, it is not, 'In the great tradition of Tolstoy or Dostoevsky' (clever though that 'or' is). Nor is it, as another reviewer gushed, 'simply about bigness'.

The most interesting things about *S,M,L,XL* can be simply

stated. In descending order of significance they are follows. (1) The title, which is so brilliant that it sells the plot to people who have not seen it and cannot afford to buy it, as well as potential readers. Given space one could write a dissertation on the significance of this title as a book in microform. Suffice to say it is as successful and meretricious a title as *Small is Beautiful*, and that is saying something. (2) Size and shape. S,M,L,XL looks like a book, but not like your average run of the mill architecture book (big pix small print, no brain). Instead it looks like a cross between a parts catalogue on a trade counter and a family bible. This too is a triumph. Most coffee table books are decorative accessories: this one is a decorative imperative. It cries out to be the only book in the house. (3) Contents. Here we run into shoals. One picayune reader, still picking his way through the end papers, found incontrovertible evidence that although the Office for Metropolitan Architecture was founded in 1975 it already had 10 staff in 1972. Another objected to Koolhaas's endless running list of *bons mots* because it included great chunks of unacknowledged Kurt Vonnegut and Tom Wolfe. A third admired the terse comment on China's future; 'Two billion people *won't* be wrong'. A fourth chuckled at the account of Japanese meetings; 'Nobody leaves the room before 300 decisions are made'. A fifth thought the legs of the Saint Cloud house looked like a stork. A sixth searched in vain for plaudits for Matthias Ungers or Alvin Boyarsky. A seventh thought recent articles in *Architecture New York* about Edith Farnsworth and Mary Tyler Moore had been triggered by Koolhaas's fantasy about the Barcelona Pavilion. An eighth (and the last) thought of Buckminster Fuller and weighed the book. It weighs 2.27 kg. Guaranteed six times as much as any other book.

PERFECT INSIGHT

The Renzo Piano Logbook. Preface by Kenneth Frampton. Thames & Hudson, London 1997.

It is a truth universally acknowledged that an architect of a certain age, universally admired, with an awesome portfolio of magnificent projects to his name, must be in want of a biographer. What is less universally acknowledged is that the biography that results is generally unsatisfactory. The graphic design is impressive of course, and the photographs and drawings are excellent – are there such things as bad photographs these days? – but the over-long introduction to the volume is anodyne, bearing the laundry marks of many hands, eager to wash away the slightest speck of controversy. Worst of all are the project descriptions, for project description writing has become a sub-species of architectural writing that is beneath contempt. Virtually unreadable, either because it is allotted a microscopic type size, or because the information it contains has been translated into (or out of) gibberish, or through plain lack of knowledge or interest, it serves the subjects of most biographies ill.

The finest quality of *The Renzo Piano Logbook* is that, at a stroke, it avoids these evils. The introduction may be soporific but it is mercifully short, and the rest of the book is given over to excellent narrative project descriptions written by, or with, Renzo Piano himself. These essays, some 58 of them covering work from 1966 to the present, are reflective, insightful and beautifully translated. Many are like tiny short stories, unhurried, filled with knowledge, wisdom and experience, in every way a joy to read.

Interestingly enough Piano, who was born in Genoa in 1937, the son of a builder, maintains that this background alone saved him from delusions of grandeur. 'Thanks to my father', he once told a Japanese journalist, 'I have what you might call antibodies against impractical nonsense'.

These 'antibodies' benefit this volume greatly. According to his own narratives – there is a co-writing credit for Roberto Brignolo – they enable Piano to announce cheerfully that he has 'no neuroses at all', and they enable him to continue to pace himself for a long career that has continually expanded in scale and expertise since he first began experimenting with lightweight geometrical structures in plywood and plastics. More obviously they have enabled him to continue to develop his famous Piano Building Workshop in Genoa into neither an office, nor a laboratory, nor a factory, but a unique evolutionary facility that lives in a world of its own somewhere between all three, engaging in work on the other side of the world – where it designed the terminal for Japan's $7 billion Kansai airport – as easily as it has done on the metro system for downtown Genoa.

As this book makes clear, much of Piano's uniqueness stems from his involvement with non-architectural projects. In 1978, in association with the late Peter Rice, Piano drew up designs for a small truck called the 'Magic Carpet' that was intended for use in developing countries. The main structural element of the vehicle was a ferrocement chassis to be made locally. Now, at a distance of 20 years, he reflects; 'It had everything that it should have, but it did not satisfy the need for modernity of which the automobile is an expression'.

Like his former colleague Richard Rogers, Renzo Piano's international career began with the competition win that allowed them jointly to design the Centre Pompidou in Paris, the most successful public building of the second half of the 20th century. He followed this great success with work for large corporations like Fiat, Schlumberger and IBM, as well as renovation and refurbishment work in Venice, new buildings in North Africa and work for international agencies like UNESCO, exercising a creativity that melds all he has learned into a force for good.

THE SPLENDOUR OF REYNER BANHAM

A Critic Writes: Essays by Reyner Banham. Selected by Mary Banham, Paul Barker, Sutherland Lyall and Cedric Price. Foreword by Peter Hall. University of California Press, San Francisco 1997.

'The splendour (and misery) of writing for dailies, weeklies, or even monthlies, is that one can address current problems currently, and leave posterity to wait for the hardbacks and PhD.

dissertations to appear later.' So wrote Reyner Banham in the foreword to a collection of his magazine articles selected by Penny Sparke and published in 1981. 'The misery and splendour of such writing, when it is exactly on target', he went on, 'is to be incomprehensible by the time the next issue comes out'.

The distance in time and attitude between that anthology and this one is instructive. Peter Reyner Banham died in 1988 so the oldest of the 54 articles reprinted here was penned nearly half a century ago. Clearly we are deep into hardback and PhD time already. But the PhD-ification of Reyner Banham is clearly having peculiar results. This volume, for example, is a curiously sanitized production, typographically and designwise austere, and heavily dosed with section introductions that are as doleful as the stations of the cross. What does this unfamiliar context do to Banham's much-admired writing? Well, for a start, the diminutive sans serif type face and the deracination of the original illustrations make it, for the first time in its life, rather a hard read. The articles that once jazzed up the pages of *Architectural Review* and *Art in America* now look as uninviting as court transcripts. And oh, so long! Did a typical magazine article really push 3000 words back in the 1960s and 1970s? Apparently it did. One might also quibble with the selection of pieces – why on earth was the seminal 'A Home is not a House' left out? But there is more to it than that. The truth is that the journalistic morning-after incomprehensibility Banham welcomed in 1981 plays curious tricks in 1997. Many of the pieces that bowled along in a jolly fashion in the 1960s, run a little flat in the grim anti-technological backlash of the pre-Millennium.

All of this means that *A Critic Writes* resembles a book of footnotes, rather than a book, a primer to some other immense volume that has been lost and nowadays exists only in the mind. This lost masterpiece, comprising the enormous oeuvre and the wonderful insights, the memorable lecturing style and the eccentric wardrobe of Reyner Banham, the greatest English optimist of the 20th century, is gone the way of the great library of Alexandria. It will not be conjured back into existence by such academic sobriety as this.

A MAN FOR ALL SEASONS

Colin Davies. *Michael Hopkins: The Work of Michael Hopkins and Partners*. Phaidon, London 1993.

The architecture of Michael Hopkins covers a multitude of sins – in the eyes of non-architects that is. For years a devoted Modernist, committed to prefabrication, finished-assembly construction and see-through aesthetics, with the waning of the century he has trimmed his sails to a new wind and became a materials fundamentalist instead. Today he rolls easily in a gentle swell, sails aback, waiting for the rest of the field to catch him up. And the wait will do him no harm, for his office is loaded to the gunwales with major establishment commissions. On the drawing boards in Marylebone is every variety of fundamentalist building you can imagine, from non-air-conditioned derivatives of the Inland Revenue Offices at Nottingham (which replaced the risible efforts of an earlier design and build team), to the new water-cooled Parliamentary Building at Westminster (which will, with its Piranesian Jubilee Line station underneath, finally replace the luckless 1970s *grand projet* of Robin Spence and Robin Webster).

This book, in a remarkably clear and straightforward fashion, sets forth the entire history of Michael Hopkins' architecture. Not quite a large-type edition, it is nonetheless so easy to browse through or read that one almost feels guilty gaining an appreciation of such impressive buildings with so little effort. Nor is the clarity solely pictorial. Colin Davies' introduction is a model of straightforward narrative that provides just enough childhood background and student life before plunging into the only navigable passage there is between the young Michael Hopkins of Foster Associates, Green King and Patera, to the middle aged Michael Hopkins of Glyndebourne and Bracken House.

Whatever one thinks of Michael Hopkins' architecture, it has undoubtedly been his capacity to shift in and out of high-tech architecture that has set him apart from the rest of his generation. Hopkins plays fast and loose with history, not only seeking inspiration in the Renaissance, but commissioning a retired architectural photographer to give a 'forties feel' to pictures of some of his buildings. Yet at the same time his credentials as a Modernist are impeccable. He and his wife Patty not only raised their family and ran their office from a glass and steel box in Hampstead, they erected another one in Marylebone when they moved their office out of the house. Today Hopkins feels no call to defend the Modern canon when it comes under attack. Instead the key he offers to inspirational flexibility is 'honesty'. As the book shows us, the Edwardian brick arches at Lords are just as real as the steel tubes and cables at mast-supported Schlumberger.

To some extent this makes sense, but neither Colin Davies, nor Patrick Hodgkinson, nor Kenneth Frampton (all of whom have essays in this book) ever really explores the uncertainties underlying the exhumed building technology of this neo-Victorian functionalism. After all, the 'chimneys' on the Parliamentary building are only real in the sense that they are working types of heat exchanger, they are not the bona fide 19th century smokestacks they appear to be.

FIVE

Victims

Comprehensive redevelopment, London 1966. Source: Author.

Our actions, our enterprises, our illnesses less and less result from objective motivations; more often they result from a violent distaste for ourselves . . . which leads us to release our energies in a form of exorcism.

Jean Baudrillard 1986

GRUDGES LONG HELD

Niels Prak. *Architects: The Noted and the Ignored.*
Wiley, New York 1984.

Niels Prak, a professor at the University of Delft, is not as well known in this country as he might be. Unlike Aldo van Eyck or even John Habraken, he has not made the leap from the insightful isolation of the mainland European languages to the global reach and empty word-processing of English language architectural culture. But for years he has been devouring the mass pulpography of English language magazines, puzzling out the bizarre proof-reading of multi-language annuals and asking himself the crucial question. Why are some architects famous and others not? From common observation of architectural practice, this is a matter of some importance. Why was Lister Fellender singled out for stardom? Why had nobody ever heard of John Poulson until he was dragged into court – even though he ran the largest architectural firm in England?

Prak's answers to these questions are more complicated than they might appear at first sight. He argues that a conspiracy of critics, historians and 'artistic' architects is what creates 'stars', and these 'stars', by dint of publishing books and lecturing about their work, influence the designs executed by their anonymous brethren 'bogged down in the harsh realities of the building industry: the price per cubic foot, the resale value, the reluctance of developers to experiment' and so on.

So far so obvious, but Prak believes that the traffic is not all one-way. The profession's leaders are not merely copied but *hunted*. Stardom in architecture, like stardom in Hollywood, leads to hubris, self-parody and, ultimately, disaster. The expectations of followers drive on the leaders until they find themselves in the defects liability court or up before the risk assessor. Fame, quite directly, brings ruin: and then the fickle crowd turns elsewhere and follows someone else. The masters of yesteryear languish in obscurity – as indeed do the surviving masters of modern architecture today.

As even this brief description makes clear, almost no one could write a boring book on such a theme – and Prak is no exception. His chapters on Mies van der Rohe's horrendous style of teaching in Chicago, on the evolution of the profession in the 20th century, on the difference between the utopianism of the 1920s and the utopianism of the 1940s, all make absorbing reading despite their rigorously academic style.

'To believe in a futuristic utopia', writes Prak in his introduction, 'you have to believe in the future itself. This belief is influenced by circumstances. In the 1930s, as today, increasing unemployment and the growing threat of war made belief in the future wane . . . This became visible, then as now, in a growing nostalgia in architecture, both on the popular and the avant garde levels (e.g. la Tendenza, the Kriers, Stirling and Bofill)'.

In Prak's view the response to this crisis has provided the elite of historians and critics with a problem of their own. Because they must simultaneously differentiate themselves from each other and maintain a united front against outsiders they have been unable to find a rallying point. As in Hollywood the 'star' system is diffusing and getting out of control.

BAL TRAGIQUE A BERLIN: I SURVIVIANT

Albert Speer. *Inside the Third Reich.*
Weidenfeld & Nicolson, London 1971.

'I have a special treat for you tonight mein Fuehrer', wheezes the sycophantic Funk, 'A new film by Kenneth Anger called "Scorpio Rising".'

Albert Speer does not record the Fuehrer's reaction to Anger's sweating motor cycle maniac homosexual nazi suburbanite. Instead he returns to his desk, above which hangs a painting of Hitler on horseback, in a suit of armour, carrying a lance. The new dome in Berlin will be over 260 m high. Hmmm.

There is of course nothing funny about being jailed for 21 years, nothing funny about genocide, gas chambers or trying to conquer the world. There is not even much funny about Adolf Hitler himself – apart from a fascinating vignette of his ordering ravioli in the Osteria restaurant every day, but always studying the menu for several minutes first. On the contrary, there is much that is tragic about the kind of 'Navy Lark' writ large that emerges from the leisurely pages of Speer's book. In a macabre way one is forced to the conclusion that if Adolf and his friends had never existed, *Private Eye* might have invented them. Nonetheless there is something richly comic about the greening of Albert Speer.

Speer begins as a po-faced disciple of Tessenow, an innocent if ambitious technician and aesthete in architecture. Slowly he progresses by way of redecorating bloodstained apartments and knocking up new Chancelleries in a year to the point where his father is accorded the great honour of an introduction to Albert's powerful friend. At the meeting the father is smitten with terror and cannot speak. Thereafter Albert is on his own. Immersed in work he promises his wife a world trip in 1950 when Berlin has been rebuilt. Immense models are constructed, extraordinarily boring evenings with Hitler spent. Together, Adolf and Albert zoom about the country in a super-charged Mercedes. 'What fun we had', reminisces Adolf, 'Teasing the big American cars . . . Their motors couldn't take it; after a while they would overheat and they'd have to pull over to the side of the road looking glum. Serve them right'.

Back in the office the two chums earnestly study building plans, so much to do, so little time. Adolf has been getting bad stomach pains and fears he may not live long enough to see his plans come to fruition. Turn on the afterburner! After the conquest of France they pay a brief visit to Paris early in the morning; their guide to the Paris Opera refuses to accept a tip. Bad sign that. Later things start to go wrong in Russia and the troops begin to sing defeatist songs. Albert copies down the words and shows them to Adolf; someone gets court-martialled for that. Serve them right.

Then Dr Todt, father of the autobahn system, gets his come uppance in a plane crash and Albert is made minister of armaments. The relationship between the two friends changes at once into one of direct employment. The idea of 'Taking a few months off after the war' to study building plans is mentioned less and less often because by now things are going wrong everywhere, not just in Russia. On July 20th 1944 things even start going wrong in Rastenburg and Berlin. The good guys get strung up on meat hooks for a colour movie but the damage is done. Albert deeply immersed in the employment of slave labour and product rationalization of all kinds, begins to think ill of his erstwhile pal. When Adolf loses all his marbles and tries to burn down Germany, Albert forestalls him. He devises a neat servicing engineer death for the mad Fuehrer but unauthorized alterations to the height of a ventilation stack thwart his murder bid. It may even be that Adolf knows, but there are no hard feelings. A limp handshake and goodbye as the roof falls in on the Third Reich. Adolf gets married and blows his brains out at the age of 56: Albert is taken into captivity at the age of 40. 'I suppose you'll be writing your memoirs now', invites an American guard.

The client relationship thus terminated, Albert Speer spends the next 21 years reading and thinking in horrifying isolation in Spandau prison. The scales fall from his eyes and he sees through the ghastly architectural equation 'Human needs = Client's requirements' once and for all. Against all the odds a major consciousness expansion takes place and the old man who leaves prison in the year of the miniskirt looks with quizzical shame upon the Wagnerian figure who went in during the year of the prefab. Because of this enforced removal from the centre of events, Albert's book is the product of a time lock of 20 years. These are not the reminiscences of an old man at all, they are the current preoccupation's of ghost. A ghost who only left the Third Reich 3 years ago as the doors of Spend prison closed behind him. For this reason, as much as any other, *Inside the Third Reich* shows us the fallacy of history more clearly than any other book on this astonishing period. It shows us clearly that history is a mirror image. Instead of seeing the progression en-classic architecture, Hofbrau House, Party rally, Greater Germany, world conquest, repulse, guided missile, genocide – we see precisely the reverse. Now we try to argue that neo-Classic architecture is caused by genocide, instead of arguing the reverse. Both efforts are fatuous in any case, for even if we prove that we know that 260 m domes lead to extermination, we have only raised questions about our own world. We have the Lincoln Centre, the Astrodome, Centrepoint . . . Where are our extermination camps? Perhaps the Yippies are in line for them.

The awful truth about architecture and dictatorship is contained in the excellent French proverb which says when a thief is not actually stealing he considers himself an honest man. Until Speer heard the evidence at the Nuremburg trials about the Jewish family going to their deaths – evidence that he maintains will haunt him for the rest of his life – he was simply an architect who got lots of super jobs from a client who happened also to be a friend, a gifted amateur, and a man who respected professionalism. And one thing about Albert Speer is an absolute certainty – he was, and is, a professional.

Albert Speer's first career (1933–1945) was a microcosm of the role of the architect in the 20th century; beginning as a traditionalist neo-Classicist he became a functionalist, an industrial designer, a systems engineer and an administrator. The long dark night of Speer's second career (1947–1967) may well reflect the eclipse of old, discredited and ridiculed architectural the – an event that is already well under way. His third life (1967–?) is way ahead of us. It poses an insoluble conundrum.

SIC TRANSIT GLORIA MUNDI

Gordon E. Cherry and Penny Leith. *Holford: A Study in Architecture, Planning and Civic Design.* Mansell, London 1986.

This is a book that will not be widely read, nor probably even widely reviewed, but it is nonetheless an important document of architectural history and an object lesson in the ephemerality of architectural reputation. William Graham Holford, Baron Holford of Kemp Town, 1907–1975, was an architect and planner of enormous power and influence in the world of post-war reconstruction. He rose to prominence in England at the same time as Modern architecture and the concept of town and country planning that accepted comprehensive urban redevelopment as a matter of course, and indeed he played a key role in the evolution of modern planning law as enshrined in the 1947 Town and Country Planning Act. A master politician in the professional sphere and a lifelong advisor to the English establishment, he became president of the Royal Institute of British Architects and the Royal Institute of Town Planning and received the Royal Gold Medal of both institutions. So great was his professional stature at the time of his RIBA Gold Medal investiture that he received his medal from the hands of Her Majesty the Queen herself at a half-hour private audience. Holford played an important part in the post-war planning of the City of London, and also Durban, Canberra, Cambridge and Corby. He served for a quarter of a century on the Royal Fine Art Commission and for 15 years on the Central Electricity Generating Board. As an architect he was responsible for university buildings at Canterbury and Exeter, and major buildings at Eton and Tonbridge schools.

Yet despite all these honours and achievements Holford, as Cherry and Leith point out in this detailed and honest biography, left little behind him by way of influence and no architecture of merit, less perhaps than any other Royal Gold Medallist. Was this because the world changed so dramatically after his death that what were seen as his virtues became invisible within 10 years? Or was it because he was 'An accomplished charlatan whose speed of thought, fluency and superb dramatic gifts concealed a fundamental lack of substance and of practical grasp' – as the authors ask? Sympathetic though it is, Cherry and Leith's portrait of the man tends towards the latter answer. 'No one ever gets through a door behind Holford', they quote an anonymous associate on an early page. After giving a detailed account of his work as head of research at the newly formed Ministry of Town and Country Planning, and equally detailed accounts of the planning scandals of Saint Paul's and Piccadilly Circus, they conclude that Holford's consummate diplomatic skills masked a fundamental lack of commitment to any of the Modernist ideals for which he was the figurehead. 'Of all the things he designed or built during his lifetime', they conclude, 'he was himself his best piece of work'.

Letters and reminiscences from Holford's student years at Liverpool and at the British School in Rome make the early chapters of this book more lively than later ones, but that is in part because the authors succeed so well in evoking the atmosphere of the inter-war years. One brief and hardly credible episode conveys the remoteness and immediateness of this period perfectly. Holford is attending a theatre performance in Rome in 1931 and detects the presence of Benito Mussolini in the audience. Between acts they exchange words in a corridor; 'How are you', says the dictator, 'and how is your gallant English pound?'

ARCHITECTURE: AN OLD FRIEND REMEMBERS

Paul Shepheard. *What is Architecture? An Essay on Landscapes, Buildings and Machines.* MIT Press, Cambridge, MA 1994.

Nothing so becomes this book as its cover, a beautiful photograph of nine jets in formation over the pyramids, by courtesy of British Aerospace Military Aircraft Division. It tells you immediately that Paul Shepheard isn't a Prince of Wales parrot or even an onward and upward Modernist (if any still exist). No, he is something else. He is a spinner of tall tales. The first 20 pages of his laid back but muscular prose confirms it, he is one of those magnificent machines in a flying man like Lloyd Grossman or Godfrey Smith, a humanoid blissfully at ease while others squirm in agonies of embarrassment. Throughout the episodic passages of this book – how wise it was of Shepheard to eschew entrees in favour of endless hors d'œuvres, sweet as the gourmet menu at Le Manoir – his readers follow him like a camera crew trailing a TV personality. Not that Shepheard is an explorer in the outback.

His territory is the city and its groves of academe, and his trade is looking at familiar things in an unusual way. He segues endlessly from quadrangle to street cafe to small flat to lecture hall to the great overarching hills to the North, talking all the while about pictures of nuclear submarines, memories of the AA school, flamenco, cathedrals, Brunelleschi, space shuttles and chase planes, Sir Isaac Newton and so on until he meets his match in the 625-line TV image of Sir Richard Rogers holding forth on another screen on the necessity of having the lifts on the outside of the Lloyd's building instead of the inside, so that they can be replaced without disturbing the underwriters' gloomy contemplations within. 'What about the escalators?', shouts Shepheard at an unseeing Rogers. 'They are inside, don't they have to be replaced too?' He is right of course. They do. Rogers is talking nonsense, just as he does when he blithely disregards statistical evidence and insists that cities are wonderful places to which people are returning in droves so they can walk instead of drive and meet up in parks and cafes to enjoy intellectual chat with old friends and, more or less, live like Paul Shepheard.

Shepheard's electronic encounter with Sir Richard Rogers is not typical. The reader soon forgets it, borne along on the bosom of the author's seductive prose in constant expectation that the title question will be answered somewhere among his good-tempered ramblings about the significance of London buses, the colour of sauce bottles, the faulty construction of tower blocks, the lie of the land, the importance of the Wright brothers, the fate of a monk condemned to dwell in a sphere, the attraction of this or that exquisite plaza and campo or, above all, somewhere in the wit and wisdom of his old friends 'Conrad', 'Sally' and 'Bob' with whom Shepheard frequently discusses life, the universe and everything. Somehow the impression of impending revelation, albeit growing increasingly tenuous, survives right up to page 95 when, suddenly, a different kind of old friend appears.

'Well, you old fucker', cries his old friend Terry, with refreshing candour, 'still solvent after all these years?'. The shock is palpable. Like a bolt of lightning it reveals that the only question we any longer want Shepheard to answer is exactly that. How is it that he is still solvent after all these years?

Alas, Shepheard is not to be caught out. Quick as Lloyd Grossman he bamboozles the insightful Terry into telling his own story instead. Terry, it seems, used to be a builder but has spent the last two years in prison, voraciously consuming books on architecture. Hope flickers briefly into life. How brilliant! It must be Terry, fresh from the great university of life, who is going to reveal to us what architecture is. No such luck. Terry's appearance is brief. Despite his brilliant opener, he has only been written in to ask a couple of put-up questions about whether the great Cathedrals are architecture or not. Turns out they are not. Pity.

THE TALE OF THE TOWER BLOCK

Miles Glendinning and Stefan Muthesius. *Tower Block: Modern Public Housing in England, Scotland, Wales and Northern Ireland.* Yale University Press, New Haven, CT 1993.

On the morning of Thursday, May 16th 1968, Miss Ivy Hodge went into the kitchen of her council flat to make a pot of tea. Miss Hodge lived on the 18th floor of a 22-storey tower block in the East End of London. When she struck a match to light her gas cooker an explosion knocked her unconscious. The explosion also blew out two concrete walls and brought down the concrete floor above. This caused two more walls and the floor above them to fall down too. Within seconds, the accumulated weight had caused the progressive collapse of the whole of one corner of the building. Because most of the occupants of the flats were still in their bedrooms, outside the zone of collapse, only four people were killed.

Miss Hodge's flat was in a tower block called Ronan Point, one of five on the Freemason Estate in South Canning Town. No sooner had Ronan Point been evacuated than the Labour MP for the constituency called for a public inquiry. Convened under a QC assisted by two eminent engineers, its report exculpated the designers and builders of the block, and everybody else except Miss Hodge, who had allowed her gas cooker to be connected to the mains by a helpful neighbour instead of an employee of the Gas Board. In the judgment of the inquiry inspector, the defective gas installation in Miss Hodge's flat was the sole cause of the explosion and the explosion the sole cause of the collapse. After the gas supply to all the tower blocks had been disconnected, the missing corner of Ronan Point was replaced in reinforced concrete, and three more 22-storey tower blocks of the same design were built on the estate, with additional steel reinforcement.

In the years that followed the partial collapse at Ronan Point, the event became a milestone in the politics of housing and the decline and fall of Modern Architecture. In its own way it was the housing equivalent to the disasters that had wiped out Britain's lead in air travel in the previous decade. In the 1950s the debacle of the Avro Tudor, an airliner given to crashing without trace, and the series of de Havilland Comet crashes that caused the humiliating withdrawal from service of the world's first jet airliner, had dealt British civil aviation a blow from which it never recovered. Industrialized building, another 'new technology', never recovered from Ronan Point.

Over 200 ft tall and containing 110 flats, Ronan Point was assembled from prefabricated concrete panels. The panels were lifted into position by crane and held together by bolts, rather like a giant house of cards. The system was of Danish origin but the English blocks were taller than their Danish prototypes. Nonetheless it had been in use in Denmark since 1948 and was considered a success. When Ronan Point was built it was licenced for use by 22 contractors in 12 different countries. Only in England was it ever considered to be dangerous.

Despite the emollient results of the public inquiry and the overshadowing of the month of May 1968 by more famous events elsewhere, the collapse at Ronan Point was not forgotten. By a supreme irony it had taken place at the apogee of new house construction in Britain. No less than 470 000 new flats and houses had been completed in the previous year, the largest number ever recorded. But the charismatic nature of the collapse – a dawn explosion followed by the coming apart of a 200-ft concrete house of cards – lit a fuse under the whole principle of the mass production of housing. Ever since the end of World War Two British housing policy had been about production. In the 1950s and the 1960s housing 'starts' and housing 'completions' were headline news, like interest rate changes and unemployment figures today. Ronan Point was a typical product of the post-war 'production' environment. Like all high-rise housing its construction was subsidized by central government to combat suburban sprawl. In those days, when house building was not so much a market as a mixture of social service and heavy industry, the idea of council housing off the production line was as much a vote-getter as mortgage subsidized investments-for-living-in were to become 20 years later.

Despite today's popular wisdom, architects were seldom directly involved in high-rise system building. It was considered to be an engineering specialty, more appropriate to large contracting firms. Nonetheless architects had been the first to visualize tower blocks. Their ideas, that were eventually to surface in thousands of Ronan Point-like towers all around the world, were born in the 19th century and all but perfected before the Second World War. An almost exact prototype was built at Drancy, on the outskirts of Paris, in 1938. There the tall towers, low blocks and unkempt park land of the 1960s British high-rise council estate were all present. The 'Cite de la Muette', as Marcel Lods design at Drancy was called, was intended to be the first phase of a high-rise town for 20 000 persons.

Because of their shared responsibility for the high-rise vision and because 30 years ago they were far more heavily immersed in public sector work than they are today, the collapse at Ronan Point was a severe blow to the prestige of Britain's architects. In 1968 half the profession worked for local authorities, producing 'social architecture' of all kinds – schools, hospitals and housing. They were, as Miles Glendinning and Stefan Muthesius, the authors of *Tower Block*, remind us, idealists, 'the aristocracy of the profession'. How hard these idealists took the attacks on the principle of high-rise that followed Ronan Point can be seen by the way their leading weekly magazine, *The Architects' Journal*, covered the story. There was a full account of the partial collapse in the news section the week after it occurred, but this was accompanied by a story about the designer of Balfron Tower, a 26-storey Poplar high-rise, the tallest local authority tower block in England, who had volunteered to live with his wife in a flat on the top-floor. 'I have made friends with all of them', the architect was reported as saying of his fellow tenants, while his wife spoke warmly of her 'new friends' and the mothers who 'love the flats'.

Outside professional circles, the media took a different view. Like Prince Charles' much later Hampton Court speech attacking architects, the story of the collapse at Ronan Point illuminated a sitting target. A quarter of a century after the event, journalists were still seeking out aged designers and promoters of tower blocks for interviews. From being harbingers of a new world, the tower blocks slowly evolved into symbols of a nightmarish confidence trick played by 'experts'.

'EE IT WERE UTOPIA'

Peter Mitchell. *Memento Mori: The Flats at Quarry Hill, Leeds.* Smith Settle, Otley 1990.

Sometimes it seems as though the sole question of the hour is whether money can be raised to preserve the great buildings of the Modern Movement like Gothic Cathedrals or demolish them as though they were old Nissen huts. Today it diverts the Thirties Society, English Heritage and Docomomo in much the same way as estimates of the number of angels that could dance on the head of a pin diverted medieval divines. But for all this agonizing, in the end it is history that supplies the answer, not another conference, another bureaucracy and another report. Buildings are destroyed by accident or demolished for entirely unpredictable reasons. Who could have foreseen the destruction of medieval stained glass by the iconoclasts? The wholesale destruction of architecture by serial bombardment? The demolition of the great battleship public housing projects of the Modern Movement – before they were even paid for – to the accompaniment of public glee?

The contribution of Leeds photographer Peter Mitchell's book *Memento Mori* to this whole question of the death and transfiguration of buildings is beyond price. Its cover picture alone, showing a demolition crew posing beneath the last arch of Quarry Hill flats in Leeds on May 22nd 1978, is an image-monument to the epic of public housing in the 20th century more poignant even than the well-known movie of Pruitt-Igoe blowing up. Inside its covers the book is much, much more. A complex, diffuse and obsessive scrapbook of images and information about the 938 unit complex of flats that in 1936 was to have been merely the first phase of a 5000 unit behemoth of Leeds, 'the largest municipal centre in Europe', designed by city architect R. A. H. Livett along the lines of the Karl Marx Hof in Vienna.

In the event the steel-framed, precast concrete-clad 'advanced technology' settlement, with its 'dustbin-free' Garchey waste disposal systems, restaurant, shops, bank, laundry and recreational facilities – a complex declared in 1955 to be suitable for 'atomic heating' – was never extended according to this grand design. Completed in 1939, the years of wartime neglect and postwar austerity told upon the fabric of the first phase and by the 1960s it was claimed to be too large and expensive to maintain. A £350 000 facelift made no difference. By 1970 when Diana Dors starred in a TV series filmed at Quarry Hill, an elevated road had already been built only 20 ft from one of its long facades. In 1975 the decision was taken to evacuate and demolish the whole complex: a process that Mitchell's beautifully designed book with its haunting photographs, serendipitous press cuttings and reminiscences of another age, captures with the perfection of a time capsule.

NOT FOR THE FAINTHEARTED

Architectural Competitions 1792–1949 (Volume I) and 1950–today (Volume II). Edited by Cees de Jong and Erik Mattie. Benedikt Taschen, Cologne 1995.

The saga of the Cardiff Bay Opera House, wherein efforts were made to rob the competition winner of her commission by means of an unscheduled re-running of the final stage, serves to remind us of the way of the world in architecture. While at first sight it might seem utterly fair and democratic that architects should compete for major public commissions, and probably private commissions as well, in practice things seldom work out quite so equitably. For example, when a competition is thrown open to all, the judges may drown in a deluge of entries (over 600 in some cases), few of which will be from architects of repute, for they fear the humiliation of losing. Conversely, when a competition is limited to a small number of well-known names, the cry goes up that new talent is being deliberately excluded. Nor is the administration of architectural competitions above reproach. In some open competitions the admission fees have totalled more than the prize money, making the exercise a kind of embezzlement. In so-called 'ideas' competitions, all the ideas produced by all the entrants are immediately available to the promoters and can easily be adopted without the formality of appointing the architect who thought of them. For reasons like these, in the real world, architectural competitions have become as much engines of controversy, ill-feeling and injustice as incubators of genius. In Britain, where architectural competitions have been much less frequent in the 20th century than the 19th, not many architects look forward to the prospect of the coming Europe-wide level playing field of universal public sector competitions. They fear a rash of foreign winners, starting perhaps with the Swiss team recently commissioned to transform Bankside power station.

Sentiment to the contrary, the tender feelings of architects are not the only consideration where competitions are concerned. However brilliant, the competitors themselves are no more than actors in a drama. The audience is the public and ultimately civilization itself. One is reminded of this fact, leafing through the very reasonably priced cased volumes of *Architectural Competitions 1792–Today*, with their tri-lingual text (English, French and German), and their beautifully designed and printed pages. Without fuss, this objective record of 50 famous competitions makes the opposite case for the value of architectural competitions with tremendous force. On the basis of buildings that have become household names alone – the Reichstag in Berlin (twice), the Houses of Parliament in London, the Eiffel Tower, Stockholm City Hall, the Sydney Opera House, the Centre Pompidou, the Hongkong and Shanghai Bank, the Carre d'Art at Nimes . . . Fair or unfair, architectural competitions have brought forth virtually all the great designs, built or unbuilt, of the last two centuries. From the nine American architects who competed to design the White House in Washington, DC, to the 681 from all over the world who contested the commission for the Centre Pompidou in Paris, competing architects have literally made history.

Apart from the superb collection of images in these two volumes, their most interesting feature is the feast of half-forgotten competition stories that the editors' admirably terse descriptions of each contest throws up. 'Tragedy is a part of architecture', as the introduction solemnly observes, but tragedy in the arts often flirts with black comedy. Consider the case of the competition to design the Law Courts in London, the most expensive public building of the Victorian era. This begins with a political row about the selection of the judges – one of them is Gladstone himself – and ends with the commission being offered to two separate contestants, then being withdrawn from both, then being offered to a contestant who accepts it, but dies before his design is executed.

Scarcely more edifying is the story of the Eiffel tower. Having cooked up with engineer Gustave Eiffel (whose office has already prepared detailed drawings) the idea of building the world's first 300 m tower as the centrepiece of the forthcoming 1889 Paris exhibition, the French Minister of Trade announces an open architectural competition for its design – closing date 17 days later! Miraculously there are 107 entries, most of which give in to the inevitable and either only indicate where such a tower might stand or show Eiffel's own design next to their own version of the exhibition buildings. Unsurprisingly the winner is Eiffel's own architect Stephen Sauvestre.

MUCH ADO ABOUT NIHIL

Massimo Cacciari. *Architecture and Nihilism: On the Philosophy of Modern Architecture.* Yale University Press, New Haven, CT 1993.

'This book', observes Massimo Cacciari, professor of aesthetics at the University of Venice, 'brings together my most significant essays on certain aspects of modern architecture viewed in the light of aesthetic-philosophical problematics'. The light cast by this polysyllabic lantern is dim. Architecture, a profession which is elsewhere rapidly becoming consumerized, clearly retains its mystery in the groves of Italian academe, where Maldonado, Cacciari, Tafuri, Francesco Dal Co and others of the Asti Spumante Left relentlessly agree with one another about the past.

The subject of Cacciari's essays is the inner essence of Modern Architecture, but there is no narrative to point the way to the target area. In Italy, as in Britain, the identification of Modern Architecture with Socialism set the stage for years of state monopoly Modernism after World War Two, but at the same time posed great difficulties for later historians. As a result, now that the once widespread pride in the impulse that produced schools and universities, hospitals and housing instead of churches and palaces, has faded from living memory, Modern Architecture is increasingly seen only in art historical terms, as a great and increasingly inexplicable heresy: a cultural revolution that burst out and took nearly a century to cram back into its box.

The beneficiaries of the Modern mutiny, the generation of 1945, acceded to a dizzy spin-doctor status unvisited by the profession since the time of the Pharoahs. They became accustomed, as a matter of course, to being called in by such potentates as the presidents of France and Brazil and the Shah of Iran, to modernize their countries, build new capital cities, tame smokestack industries and house the poor and huddled masses.

The status of these men, whose names are all but forgotten, was awesome. In 1945, within days of the end of the war in Europe, the US Army placed Hans Scharoun, who

had designed no more than a few houses in Germany before
the war, in charge of the replanning of Berlin. In his memoirs the English architect and town planner Max Lock
records, as late as the 1960s, changing into native robes
whenever his plane prepared to land in a newly independent
African country, all the better to acknowledge the adulation
of the populace. Sir William Holford, the now execrated
planner of the environs of St Paul's Cathedral, enjoyed the
special distinction of an hour-long audience with the Queen,
when he was knighted for his services to architecture in
1971.

It is the philosophical underpinnings of this great triumph
that Massimo Cacciari is writing about in this book of essays.
But his poorly translated and impenetrably elided prose casts
little light upon it for the general reader. This is revisionist
commentary, not readable narrative. Instead of a crusade
begun by giants and frittered away by pygmies, Cacciari's
Modern era is a philosophical conundrum awash with
nihilism from birth. Of course cities, towns, history and communities were destroyed by Modern Architecture, he says with
the benefit of hindsight, everybody knows that;

> The architecture 'without qualities' of the metropolis is a con-
> scious image of fulfilled nihilism. Every place is equi-valent in uni-
> versal circulation. Space and time are a-rithmetically measurable,
> detachable, and reconstructible.

In other words Modernism is still succeeding, in an unsuccessful sort of way, especially where ignorant people think it
most conspicuously failed. And so too does the medium of
one age become the tedium of the next, as Marshall
MacLuhan predicted. In this indigestible monstrosity of a
book, in so far as there is any coherent meaning at all, there
is only a story turned on its head and a great adventure
reduced to innumerable unremarkable events. Its high point
is where, improbably but illustratively, Cacciari parodies his
own critical technique by quoting from Walter Benjamin
quoting from somebody else on the difficulty of going
through a door:

This is a very complicated undertaking. First I have to struggle against the atmosphere, which presses against my body with a force of one kilogram per square centimetre. Then I must try to set foot on a floor that is travelling at a speed of 30 kilometres per second around the sun . . . Indeed it is easier for a camel to pass through the eye of a needle than for physicist to cross his own threshold.

Confronting such difficulties nobody is a failure.

MAVERICK BRETT

Lionel Brett. *Ourselves Unknown: An Autobiography*. Gollancz, London 1985.

'Consider the plight of the children of the rich', wrote Marshall McLuhan in 1951. 'The speed, the struggle, the one-man fury are not for them.' He must have been thinking of Lionel Brett, otherwise known as Lord Esher (the Beeching of the studios), for there is throughout this beautifully written memoir evidence of a chronic weightlessness that forever throws its hero away from the centre of events despite the accident of birth that placed him at the heart of the greatest upheavals of our century.

Born before the Great War of a magical mixture of American money and English lineage, young Brett attends Eton and Oxford, and appears to have spent the 1930s enjoying an interminable series of continental holidays. 'The Hitler craze is a bore but it doesn't seem to have spoilt this part of Germany', he writes gaily from Wurzberg. 'They march about in companies singing marvellously: they woke us up singing at five'. Brett himself is perfectly content: 'In crystal air I stuff books into a rucksack, climb 4000 ft in a couple of hours and read till sunset on the tip of some peak'. On the eve of the Spanish Civil War he sits alone in an empty hotel lounge above a pounding sea in a Spanish fishing village: 'A trio with an English fiddler (who was Laurie Lee) had only me to play to'. The unlikely appearance of Lee in this sentence is but an example of the serendipitous social outreach Brett achieves throughout his narrative – an example also of the tendency for great events to take a backseat while celebrities wander in and out of the pages. In this way we make the undeveloped acquaintance of Miki Sekers, Jo Grimond, Donald Maclean, Cyril Connolly, John Betjeman, Maurice Bowra, Richard Crossman, Peggy Ashcroft, Lord Mountbatten and others.

When war comes young Brett becomes first a volunteer fireman and then a gunner – 'A drop-out from educational and social privilege' – fighting from D-day to the Elbe and ending up as a troop commander unfashionably preoccupied with the injustice of destruction while his colleagues loot their prostrate corner of Germany.

Demobilized rapidly so that he can fight the 1945 election as a Liberal, Brett comes a poor third in the poll but saves his deposit. He turns to architecture but somehow ends up as a planner instead. As he truthfully notes, 'Silly ladies meeting me for the first time still lead off with, "Oh yes, weren't you once in trouble about roofs blowing off?". It is the only thing widely known about my architectural career'. But even the Hatfield disaster is socially significant, for the young Scarman conducts the court of inquiry. As a planner Brett fights tooth and nail to keep narrow streets and a medieval town atmosphere at Hatfield, and is rewarded by Sir James Richards excluding him from *The Architectural Review*'s general denunciation of the New Towns; but even here history cheats him with universal car ownership, making the tight planning a liability. Thus it is with all Brett's planning consultancies, from Maidenhead to Caracas, Corsica to Cadogan Place.

Peering down from the standpoint of bemused self-regard that characterizes *Ourselves Unknown*, the author discourses philosophically on his children's generation as the first to have been relieved of the necessity to maintain a national purpose ('They belong to a class which had hitherto considered itself in charge not just of this country but of the world') but in general there is little intellectual speculation – Brett having shot his bolt in *Parameters and Images* and later in *A Broken Wave,* his history of the Modern Movement in Britain. Instead the reader is left with the solace of Brett's beautiful style – he is far and away the best architecture *writer* of his generation – and the fund of curious anecdotes that continue until the end, when he dispassionately describes overtaking his own mother in an ambulance on the M40, shortly before she died. It is an odd and sad book, but immensely readable.

AMERICA CAN MAKE IT

Jean-Louis Cohen. *Scenes of the World to Come: European Architecture and the American Challenge 1893–1960.* Canadian Centre for Architecture/Flammarion, London 1995.

It was probably Langdon Winner who first argued that the American Constitution of 1787 was a specification with design implications. 'If Alexis de Toqueville were visiting the United States in the late 20th century', he remarked, 'his book on its customs might well be entitled *Technology in America*'. And if de Toqueville would have thought that about America today, we might reply, after scanning Jean-Louis Cohen's fascinating book, that an American visitor to Europe might have entitled his book *Technology of America*. *Scenes of the World to Come* is the catalogue of an exhibition of the same name, on the subject American influence, that opened last summer at the Canadian Centre for Architecture in Montreal and is destined to tour the world until the year 2000.

From our vantage point today we can see that fascination with America coloured a good half century of European history, perhaps its last half century as an independent world power, before Americanism became 'Americanization'. The difference now is that Cohen asks us to change our viewpoint. Accustomed as we are to seeing American influence upon European architecture depicted as something that begins with the propaganda of Adolf Loos and Richard Neutra, swells to breaking point with the buildings of Mies van der Rohe, and finally dies away with the eclipse of the button-down brushcut organization men of Ulm and the SAR, we overlook the scale of US influence at much higher levels. As Cohen makes clear, not only did Hollywood swamp European imagination, but so did skyscraper building and mass production. After the Russian Revolution the great truck and tractor factories built in the Soviet Union in the 1920s were a homage to Henry Ford. So was Hitler's Volkswagen factory built at Wolfsburg a decade later. This is the homage that endured. In 1930 three-quarters of all Communist Russian tractors were Fords. In 1939 Nazi emissaries were still in Detroit, head-hunting German emigre automobile engineers to come home and set up the first Beetle production line. All these indicators dissolved into World War Two, an 'industrial war' fought on all sides, even in the Asia-Pacific region by Taylorized, Fordized masses. Vast numbers of workers mobilized and organized according to the needs of production systems modelled on the same American prototypes. So much for influence. By 1944 it became plain that the original worked better than the copies: the outcome of the war proved it.

Of all Cohen's insights into American influence at the mega-scale, it is his account of its waning in the 1950s that is of least interest. Apparently magnetized by the Montreal Centre's collection of back issues of the *Architectural Review*, he contents himself with examples of British enthusiasm (and irritation) with America that become increasingly superficial. But then the 1960s did mark the consummation of 'Americanization' – the age of influence was already over.

ALPHABET SOUP

Philip Cooke. *Back to the Future: Modernity, Postmodernity and Locality*. Unwin Hyman, London 1990.

Not long ago there was a paint advertisement that captured the essence of post-Modernism perfectly. It showed a typist seated on an excruciatingly uncomfortable sub-Memphis chair with a pink electric typewriter in front of her, and pastel filing cabinets and drawers with conical hats on them behind. Surrounded by screwed-up sheets of paper, the typist was no longer typing but blowing bubblegum balloons while reading a copy of *Playgirl* tucked inside a book called *Learn to Type in a Day the Nimble Fingers Way.*

No room for that sort of perception in *Back to the Future*, I am afraid, even though the brazen plagiarism of its title is thoroughly appropriate to the post-Modern consciousness. What is less appropriate is the cover picture of the Rietveld Schroder house, for there is little about architecture and a great deal about sociology in the pages that follow. Even Charles Jencks, the grand master of post-Modernism in architecture, merits only one citation in the text and nothing in the bibliography.

Philip Cooke's new thesis is that, while the post-Modern attack on Modernism for its 'Keynesianist, welfarist, Fordist' uniformity was 'valid', it was also unsuccessful. Now all the sound and fury have abated we can all see that the edifice of modernity remains intact. For this reason, Cooke believes that post-Modernism will not succeed Modernism but add new tactics to its brutal old thrust: probably by the nurture of 'localism', the 'co-operative tendencies found in post-Fordian business organization' and what he describes as 'the as yet prefigurative possibilities regarding the revival of pre-Fordist methods of delivering local welfare services'.

If the reader has difficulty with the above, he or she is not alone. Perversely, Cooke seems to see a continuum extending from the social order of Victorian England to the three-day week. Poor laws and workhouses (pre-Fordist welfare services) are vigorously stirred in along with compulsory free education, council housing and the National Health Service (post-Fordist welfare services) until all become interchangeable parts of a structure of possibility that-unlike reality itself-appears to be able to go backwards in time as easily as it can go forwards because it is all part of the grand 'project of modernity'.

Unlike Cooke's text, the utility of his argument is transparent. At a stroke, it converts the clear-cut conflict of the 1970s – post-Modernism versus Modernism – into a innocuous alphabet soup for the 1990s – post-Modernism plus

Modernism. Rather unsatisfyingly, everyone ends up having been right all along.

SCHOOLS FOR SCANDAL

Mark Crinson and Jules Lubbock. *Architecture – Art or Profession? Three Hundred Years of Architectural Education in Britain.* Manchester University Press, Manchester 1994.

In a recent issue of the magazine *Architecture New York* Colin Rowe, the doyen of North American architecture critics, described architectural education as, 'After the Russian Revolution, the two world wars, the Holocaust and Modern architecture itself, the greatest catastrophe of the 20th century'. Unhappily this comprehensive denunciation is not included in *Architecture – Art or Profession?* But had it been available at the time there can be no doubt that our two authors would have fallen upon it greedily, for it perfectly sums up their bilious view of the study of architecture that has provided each with a good part of his living since leaving school. In any case their book, whose spine is decked out with the ostrich feather imprint of the Prince of Wales's Institute of Architecture and whose pages begin with a foreword by the Prince himself – that same Prince who once denounced the 'Frankenstein professors' of the Architectural Association before going on to employ them in a Frankenstein school of his own – is not short of its own superlatives of guilt and recrimination. A glance at the introduction is enough to convince any reader that nothing remotely resembling an objective account of architectural education will adorn the pages that follow. All of which is a pity because the information gathered here is of intense though arcane interest and has certainly never been brought together from such a wide range of sources before.

Of Prince Charles's foreword much could be said. It is a classic of its kind, eliding a number of unsupported assumptions into a heap of allegedly self-evident truths before bulldozing them into a mountain of popular prejudice. Typical is its assertion that professional specialization is the cause of uniformity in the built environment and that this in turn is what makes architects remote from the concerns of ordinary people. The muddle and want of logic here is pitiable, for the truth is quite the reverse and would have served the Prince far better. Professional specialization leads not to uniformity, but to monstrous mutations like post-war high rise public housing, one of the most remarkable interventions of architecture into the landscape since the Middle Ages. It is the demystification of architecture into the enforcement of simple canons of popular taste that leads to crushing uniformity and the alienation of the professionals.

Unlike the Prince, who confines himself to stabs in the semantic darkness, the authors of the main text serve up a healthy series of chapters on the subject of architectural education. A feast of information that is spoiled only by the way in which it is continually bent to the service of their own conspiratorial preconceptions. The most powerful of these is their theory that Modernism is in reality a covert 'official system' that was developed to control the whole process of building design and construction in the years after World War Two. The scale of the threat posed by this Modern conspiracy can be deduced by the authors' reliance upon the writings of William Allen, a blameless former director of the British Building Research Station and later principal of the AA school, to provide evidence of it. With sane and rational men like Allen presented as dangerous totalitarian conspirators, Crinson and Lubbock need more than indignation to sustain their allegations, and it soon emerges that they have not got it. Their last throw, a panic-stricken 4-page postscript that babbles about the rapid collapse of the so-called 'official system' into today's anarchy in architecture, reveals the bankruptcy of their whole agenda.

Sadly, despite the relevance of its subject, there is no way that this alarmist nonsense can be related to the present state of the 40 schools of architecture in Britain, with their 9000 happy students, their bulging enrolments and their new at-a-stroke university status. In any case the attempt itself is bizarre. It has often been said that if Adolf Hitler been admitted to the Vienna School of Art, there would have been no Second World War. Surprisingly neither Crinson nor Lubbock seems to understand that, however useless it might be, architectural education is good for everyone.

REACH FOR THE FLAMETHROWER

The Education of the Architect. Edited by Martha Pollak. MIT Press, Cambridge, MA 1997.

Whenever I hear the word 'culture' I reach for my revolver. So said the late and unlamented Herman Goering according to legend. The phrase has been a warning to philistines ever since it was first reported but, aw shucks, here goes. Confronted with this inadequately bound, creaking 478-page mass of architectural culture, whose finger would not itch for the trigger of a Saturday night special?

Cast in the form of a *festschrift* in the German manner, with 18 essays dedicated to Stanford Anderson, who co-founded the Department of History, Theory and Criticism of Architecture at MIT, the portentous *Education of the Architect* is, alas, little more than a reprint wheelie bin for footnotes. In all the millions of words of text crammed between its covers, Anderson himself is only mentioned three times. Meanwhile his devoted admirers flex their academic muscles in so many other directions to such effect that, by page 478, they have mustered between them no fewer than 922 footnotes. This distinction deserves recognition. The winner by miles is Carlo Olmo whose essay 'Between tradition and innovation: Place Louis XV in Paris' racks up an incredible 119 footnotes. Next across the line is Gail Fenske, whose 'Louis Mumford, Henry-Russell Hitchcock and the Bay Region Style' claims a creditable 95, while the last podium position goes to Diane Yvonne Ghirardo whose 'Surveillance and Spectacle in Fascist Ferrara' manages a solid 80. Following these leaders is a mid-field bunch comprising

Joseph Siry with 66, Nancy Stieber with 63, Mark Jarzombek with 60, Mitchell Schwartzer with 58, Danilo Udovici-Selb with 56, Hilary Ballon with 54, Akos Moravanszky with 51, Maristella Casciato with 48, Sibel Bozdogan with 48, Nasser Rabbat with 46, then Royston Landau with 37, John Habraken with 27 and, trailing the pack, Micha Bandini with 14. Neck and neck across the line in last place are Lawrence B. Anderson and Charles Correa with none.

The fact that Charles Correa supplies the 18th and last essay in the book is no doubt the result of a shrewd editorial decision, for had his contribution 'Learning from Ekalavya' been placed first, it might have cast doubt on the compelling necessity to read all the others. In it, in a tone markedly different from that used by his scholarly colleagues, Correa recounts the student experience of seeing the Mona Lisa for the first time; 'An anticlimax? No, actually something far worse. One cannot see the Mona Lisa. One stares, but it is invisible . . . nothing registers on the mind. The layers of hype are too dense to dissolve away'. He then describes himself and three other students repairing to a coffee shop after having been shown endless slides of the Sistine Chapel: 'One of us, I think it is Jack Caldwell, says: "You know what? I don't think Michaelangelo was so great". Jack could be wrong . . . or, perhaps, right . . .'. And this essay, with its final revelation of the terrible price exacted by architectural education (I won't spoil the surprise, you can read it on page 452), is so worth reading that it is worth photocopying from the book.

AND NOW THE JUMPING UNIVERSE!

Charles Jencks. *The Architecture of the Jumping Universe*. Academy Editions, London 1995.

A couple of years ago, in the depths of winter, Charles Jencks told an interviewer that he was writing a volume to be entitled 'A Walk through the Post-Modern Pluriverse'. It would, Jencks said, be at least 400 pages long, and would deal with the whole cultural phenomenon of post-Modernism in the world. This book never appeared and the mystery of the projected 'post-Modern Pluriverse' remained unsolved until now, when the publication of *The Architecture of the Jumping Universe* – only 176 pages long instead of 400 though it is – provides us with the answer. The shortness is a tad disappointing of course, but there can be no doubt that this is, in microform, the epic of which Charles Jencks spoke all those years ago.

Because this genealogy is so certain, it is even more surprising that in its shortness, its use of graphs, charts and equations, and, most of all, its presentation of examples of his own work, *The Architecture of the Jumping Universe* represents a throwback in Jencks's authorial style of nearly 30 years. Instead of collecting examples of the work of, say, Michael Graves or, more recently, Frank Gehry, and glueing them together into a kind of ransom note with the aid of a collection of sprightly neologisms, Jencks has reverted to his 1960s role as cosmologist and seer, the role he played most perfectly in the early 'Architecture 2000'. But that was at the end of the magical decade and Jencks still felt weighed down by the centuries of architectural theory with which he had grappled as a student. Nowadays he bears this load with the ease of an Olympic weight lifter. Architectural theory is not something he has to contend with, it is part of his cultural armoury, something that he prints himself, as though it were his own currency. For Jencks architectural thought is no longer trammeled by the feats of living architects or dead white male theorists.

Lots of other things are happening in the world apart from architecture. There is plant biology, microsurgery, virtual reality and earthquake studies, there is cyberspace, art and genetics and energy questions too . . . Jencks is open to all of them. If you want a link between radio astronomy and garden furniture, Jencks is it. He has some furniture designs – 'Determinism, Purpose, Chance, Scotland 1992', 'Soliton Gates, Scotland 1993', 'Soliton Stand, Scotland 1994' – all of which look like kitchen cupboards, garden furniture or garden gates, but turn out to have meanings so deep they seem like plutonium itself. Meaning transcends the medium density fibreboard of which they are made. These objects are not lunkheaded furniture so much as cosmological artifacts. They may be less than architecture of course, but also they are somehow more, and Jencks cannot wait to explain them.

'To the left, symbolized by the kitchen clock, are those who believe in a clockwork universe . . . Marx and Freud, etc.' begins one breathless description of a set of kitchen cupboards. But it is cruel to go on, the point is clear enough. If you want Newton, you get Modernism. If you want Einstein, you get post-Modernism in the shape of the Santa Fe Institute. If you want a 'Jumping Universe' that can encompass every form of creativity from serviced floorspace to the output of architects like Gehry, Miralles and Quark, bionic heroes who work with cut-ups, ink blots, photocopiers, twigs, swirling water, photography and sloping floors, then here is a preview of it. All that it requires of its designers is that they should drive themselves mad, like painters putting up a fight against photography, by trying to design 'abstract buildings' to match the paintings of Piccasso, Braque or, better yet, Nonja, the artist chimpanzee.

SIX

Buildings

'Je Ferai des maisons comme on fait des voitures' (Le Corbusier 1960).
Robotic car production at Fiat's Mirafiore plant in the 1980s. Source: Fiat
Auto SpA.

*In dissociating light and atmosphere from the context of
the natural overall atmosphere by means of an 'almost
ethereal' barrier, ferrovitreous architecture creates a
novel condition. Light and atmosphere are now perceived
as independent qualities, no longer subject to the rules of
the natural world in which they had hitherto manifested
themselves.*

Wolfgang Schivelbusch 1977

DIPLOMATIC BAG

Adam Bartos and Christopher Hitchens. *International Territory: The United Nations 1945–1995*. Verso, London 1995.

When the headquarters of the United Nations was built after World War Two it was sited in New York, as opposed to Geneva, the home of its ill-fated predecessor, the League of Nations. Why did this happen? Because, unlike the League, the United Nations was a quintessentially Modern project and where but New York could be regarded as the first city of Modernism? So writes Christopher Hitchens at the beginning of this fascinating little book, produced to commemorate 50 years of the UN and larded with anecdotes and time capsule photographs of one of the principal architectural results of the greatest outburst of idealism to follow the 1939–1945 war.

But if the geographical location of the UN was determined by the power of skyscrapers and the thumping beat of jazz, its architectural form was not. There was already a spectacular mixed-use developers' scheme for the chosen site, designed by the architect Wallace Harrison. In a flash it was turned into a fine UN headquarters 'by means of a system of double entry bookkeeping which involved pencilling in the words "General Assembly" where an opera house had been, and "Security Council" and "Trusteeship" in place of the different auditoria'. By such simple drawing board tricks was a world institution founded. Nor was its financing more complex. The site on the East River was purchased from the original developer with a single cheque for $8.5 million signed by Nelson Rockefeller senior, who then gave the land to the UN in perpetuity. The height of the building was established in similar straightforward fashion by the year of its birth, 1945, therefore 45 storeys. Alas this pragmatism did not extend into the details of the architecture. All the delays and compromises to follow were caused by arguments about architectural symbolism, and by the unconscionably large number of architects involved: a collection of names that stretched from uninvited *spontanieros* with bees in their bonnets from all over the world; to the members of the UN 'Board of Design' representing every nation and every known architectural tendency (except perhaps the neo-Classicism recently discredited by association with the defeated Axis powers). Right at the top were Oscar Niemeyer and the three supervising architects appointed by the UN Headquarters Commission – Le Corbusier, Jan de Ranitz from the Netherlands and Nikolai Bassov from the USSR.

Despite this complicated superstructure, when the project finally went on site it encountered a spirit of goodwill seldom met with in the construction industry anywhere on our planet. Professional fees were waived, suppliers agreed to fixed prices in a period of inflation, workers worked overtime for nothing and justifiable claims for payments were allowed to drop. In artistic terms the building survived all the stylistic vicissitudes to follow. Today, 50 years later, its membership already more than doubled to 166 nations and the UN survives as an enduring monument to Modernism.

LIFE'S RIGHT, ARCHITECTURE'S WRONG

Philippe Boudon. *Pessac de Le Corbusier: 1927–1967: Etude Socio-architecturale. Collection Aspects de l'Urbanisme*. Dunod, Paris 1969.

The process of physical change analysed by Boudon in this study is fundamental to our understanding of the purpose of buildings and hence of architecture. In it he traces the history of Le Corbusier's 50 houses at Pessac, near Bordeaux, from their completion in 1926, through the 3 years of bureaucratic wrangling that passed before they were allowed to be occupied, through 40 years of modification by successive occupants, to their current (1967) state. Photographs, transcribed interviews and quotations from contemporary publications catalogue the progressive destruction of the modern identity of these buildings by the addition of pitched roofs, the blocking in of strip windows, the walling in of open ground floors, the construction of extensions in traditional styles, the addition of sunburst gates, extensive planting, the covering-in of patios, the fitting of window boxes and so on.

Written with patience and humour the book avoids much of the portentous self-accusation that generally afflicts the writings of architects and sociologists when dealing with such matters, perhaps because, in this case, the architect was not a luckless, anonymous and desperately well-meaning local authority architect's department, but the great Corbu himself, from the back of whose reputation cold steel has always tended to run off like cold water. Asked during his lifetime what he thought of the 'desecration' of his buildings at Pessac, the master characteristically replied; 'C'est toujours la vie qui a raison, l'architecte qui a tort'.

The Pessac project originated in 1920 with 10 houses built at Lege, near Pessac, for the father of Henry Fruges the 'artistes multivelent' who was later to commission the 200 houses of the 'QMF' (Quartiers Modernes Fruges), by which name the Pessac development is locally known. These houses too have suffered systematic conversion back into traditional villas at the hands of their occupants. In the event only a quarter of the projected QMF was actually built. Henry Fruges assessed the public response as follows: 'Admirateurs enthousiastes, 1%. Sympathisants, 2%. Hesitants, 2%. Stupefaits et ahuris, 40%. Convaincus que j'etais devenu fou, 55%'.

After recounting contemporary professional and lay press opinions, which appear to have been studiously neutral, the book begins its sociological investigation. A discussion between a contractor, an engineer, an interior decorator, a Prix de Rome architect, a resident, and an architect engaged in research into the direction of architecture in the future throws up a remarkable conflict. All of the participants speak freely of the 'failure' of Pessac, as evidenced by all the alterations that have taken place, but the engineer, calling Le Corbusier 'Star' and 'Fuehrer', violently attacks the architecture of the 20th century as the cause of all the alterations. He denounces concrete architecture as a wartime fad. 'Quelques chimpanzes se sont mis a crier "C'est de l'art! C'est de l'art!". En realite c'etait tout simplement une mesure anti-aerienne!'. This hypothesis is supported by the ramblings of the QMF resident who opines; 'J'ai une certain admiration . . . a voir les blockhaus . . . voyez . . . il faudrait un psychanalyste! . . . Alors les pilotis de Marseille . . . Son systeme de beton brut de decoffrage, on retrouve cette espece de force qui m'interesse dans les blockhaus'. From this and other amplifying evidence Boudon deduces that there is a link between reinforced concrete and security in the minds of both architect and building user at Pessac.

By similar methods Boudon deduces that the obturation of the room-width windows in the QMF houses (more than half have had this operation performed) results from the fantastic notion that they are old fashioned, 'pas comme on fait maintenant'. Even those who have retained their wide windows remain unsatisfied. They wanted 'une grande baie accordeon' or better still 'des petits carreaux'. The signification of the original roof gardens is even more surprising, being seen as no more than the absence of a proper roof.

Curiously enough the delicate matter of the alterations proves to be the occasion for numerous unexpected plaudits to Le Corbusier, for example; 'J'ai achete cette maison en cinq minutes: exterieurement, elle ne me plaisait pas, mais j'ai toute de suite vu les possibilites . . .'. It is generally agreed that the houses were superbly designed for modification ('Mon mari en a fait deja trente-six plans differents') and one owner is admired because he has converted his house into three separate apartments. Interestingly it emerges that the long history of ambitious DIY at the QMF goes back to the legal tangle that delayed its occupation – to evade taxation the houses were let as shells with no interior decorations.

The last discovery of the book is that the incidence of dramatic alteration, far from matching the most standardized dwellings, has in fact occurred almost exclusively in those houses already distinguished by location, type or orientation from their neighbours. Corner sites, sites adjacent to existing traditional houses and houses at the ends of rows exhibit far more extensive modification and personalization than do those surrounded on all sides by 'le style QMF'. From this the author concludes that standardization stifles creativity.

Boudon's book stirs the surface of something that is destined to revolutionize architectural criticism. In the dawning age of feedback it can be seen as a landmark, principally because it is not anti-architectural in itself. The Corbusier who emerges from the analysis of Pessac is not reduced to the status of a fool nor made to seem out of date. The fantastic pitch-roof mutations of his would-be 'machines a habiter' are composite structures over time, carrying with them the evidence of as many changes as the great Mediaeval cathedrals. Interestingly the occupants of the QMF all seem to refer to Le Corbusier as 'ce gars', which is very different to not knowing his name.

WRIGHT CAN'T BE WRONG

Judith Dunham. *Details of Frank Lloyd Wright: The California Work 1919–1974*. Thames & Hudson, London 1994.

Is there no end to our curiosity about Frank Lloyd Wright? There must have been at least a hundred books about him published in the last decade and this one, although it promises detail, in the end produces only photographs, much like all the others. Perhaps its only unique features consist in the collaboration of Eric Lloyd Wright, the patriarch's grandson, and the claim on the cover that Wright's California detailing extends up to 1974 – although the master himself died in 1959. The contribution of Eric Lloyd Wright consists of an introduction recalling the impromptu lectures given by his grandfather to the assembled apprentices at Taliesin during the last years of his life. The claim that Wright detailing persisted into the 1970s turns out to be based on only one posthumous project, the tiny Lewis N. Bell residence, a Usonian house on a hexagonal planning grid designed by Wright for a hilltop site in Los Angeles in 1940, whose construction was postponed because of the war and subsequently abandoned. In 1974 Hillary and Joe Feldman bought the plans for this house and erected it on a hill in Berkeley instead. Its detailing is sparse but comfortable in the Usonian manner, but it affords no new insight into Wright's tremendous varietal range.

How to produce a book about detailing without a single drawing in it is a trick known only to the author and publishers of this volume. No one could create more inviting interiors from such unpromising mundane materials as Wright, but his mastery of concrete blocks, fretsawn timber and plywood and stained concrete is nowhere expounded as a technical problem. Instead we are presented with intriguing problems like the stepped, cantilevered glazing of the 1948 Walker residence, overlooking Monterey Bay, Wright's only coastal California house, which is heavily illustrated but explained only by the cryptic comment that the windows open downwards. Anyone who wants to find out how, will have to pursue other methods.

DIARY OF AN EMPTY-HANDED PROSPECTOR

Reyner Banham. *The Architecture of the Well-tempered Environment*. Architectural Press, London 1969.

After a painful journey of about a month he arrived at the summit of a mountain, from the summit of which the immense expanse of the Pacific Ocean burst upon his view. Affected by the sight, and falling upon his knees, he thanked the almighty for having granted him the favour of discovering these immense regions. Descending with his companions to the sea-shore, Balboa, in full armour, having in one hand his sword and the standard of Castile in the other, stood upon the sand until, the tide ascending, the water reached his knees.

The Discovery of the Pacific
National Encyclopedia 1885

The first scene of *The Architecture of the Well-tempered Environment* opens with Reyner Banham, standing like Balboa, knee-deep in a swirling tide of mechanical servicing. He is dressed in jeans and an Ed Roth T-shirt and carries in one hand a copy of *The History of Architecture on the*

Comparative Method by Sir Banister Fletcher, and a bunch of yellowed trade catalogues in the other. Cut. Unlike Balboa who merely 'took possession' of the Pacific by instructing a notary to register its change of ownership, Banham goes for a swim in his new ocean. He never returns. All that is left on the shore is the sodden, discoloured copy of Banister Fletcher – the detritus of architectural history that he tried to do without.

This is an odd-book for the author of *Theory and Design in the First Machine Age*. Odd not only because it looks funny, with its bastard square format, greyish photographs, dull typography, art paper and wholly unsuccessful jacket design; but also because it is not a very confident piece of work. Intended at first to be 'a purely architectural history. . . Less a book about firsts than about mosts', it develops into a romance with engineers 'pursuing their eccentric and mono-maniac goals', tries 'finding them a proper place in the history of architecture' and eventually admits the possibility that the 'unprecedented history' of their activities might have brought about the 'total subservience of architecture to the goals of mechanical servicing'.

Even in his first chapter, when he is still feeling the water with his toes, Reyner Banham fears that his solitude on this unexplored shore may be illusory. Anxiously he scans the horizon for a sight of a ship on the uncharted sea. There is one, a battered hulk rusted through with inadequacies, the USS *Mechanization Takes Command* under her skipper Siegfried Geidion. Banham abruptly prepares to do battle. Geidion's monumental work on the 'anonymous history' of technology from the dawn of time to 1950 is dismissed as 'shallow and unconsidered'. The high regard in which the book is held ('in no way deserved') turns out to be based on the author's prior reputation. Within a page or two Giedion has sunk without trace. Why? Because he failed, as Banham points out, even to attack the history of electric lighting.

Comparable omissions are not hard to find in *The Architecture of the Well-tempered Environment* but Banham has armed himself against criticism from this direction by pointing out early on that his work is only 'a tentative beginning, whose shortcomings. . .will become manifest as research proceeds'. It will 'serve perhaps more to reveal existing gaps than to fill them'. The trouble is that they are both at it and the last quotation comes from the foreword to Giedion's book, not Banham's.

Anyway our intrepid explore has disposed of the interloper by the beginning of Chapter 2 and he begins his long swim in the new ocean, keeping on course by means of frequent sights on the great architectural stars aloft in the firmament. There's Frank Lloyd Wright, chewing on a straw as he relaxes on some well-placed ventilation ducting. There's the old German Peter Behrens, how old-fashioned he looks with his naked light bulbs! There's Walter Gropius, did he really design the London Playboy Club? Banham backstrokes by like a bus cruising the homes of the celluloid immortals in Beverly Hills. At one point he prepares us for a secret new star, Willis Carrier the father of air conditioning, but something goes wrong and we do not even see a photograph.

By the time we reach Chapter 10 ('Concealed Power') and Chapter 11 ('Exposed Power') Banham's stroke has become jerky and his breathing irregular, soon he is in difficulties. Discussing Louis Kahn's tormented struggle with the service towers at the Richards Memorial Laboratories in Philadelphia, he nearly lets the cat out of the bag altogether. 'The non-architect must wonder how it can be that a man so thoroughly out of sympathy with more than half the capital investment in a building of this kind should be entrusted with its design . . .'. Right, that's enough. Pull him out.

After an architectural kiss of life, Banham is sufficiently recovered to pen his last chapter. It is not full of Archigram pods, cushicles, light forms, spacecraft, walking cities or even computerized distribution centres. Instead we have a learned reference to Tom Wolfe ('a literary man, operating on the very fringes of currently acceptable culture'); some discussion of what is or was the oldest inflatable building (winner the United States Atomic Energy Commission Portable Theatre of 1959) and finally the citation of the 1961 Saint George's School, Wallasey, Cheshire, by Emslie Morgan, with its pioneering double glazed 'solar wall', as the shape of things to come.

Banham's final conclusion, both true and anticlimactic, is that 'As long as buildings remain fixed to the ground in one place, which most buildings will be for some time to come. . . Every building will continue to be an unique environmental control system'. So a new ocean does not mean a new general theory of servicing-led design after all. The reason Banham could not swim right across the Pacific was because he could not survive without that volume of Banister Fletcher after all. He tried to look at the gigantic, seething world of technological evolution without the very old and very distorting glass of architectural theory and architectural history, and failed. As a result the book turns out to be indecisive when it should have been triumphant. Reyner Banham has not yet written a worthy successor to *Theory and Design in the First Machine Age*.

THOROUGHLY MODERN MYTH

Gilbert Herbert. *The Dream of the Factory-made House*. MIT Press, Cambridge, MA 1985.

In 1946 in Columbus, Ohio, a number of aeronautical engineers from the Curtiss Wright aircraft corporation took their redundancy cheques and left the factory where they had been producing military aircraft for the American forces in World War Two. They joined the 10 million strong army of demobilized veterans only briefly, for they had a plan of their own. Combining their severance pay with post-war gratuities and personal savings, they founded the Lustron Corporation, a company that was to apply the methods of aircraft production to the housing market.

A total of $36 000 of invested capital and a loan of $37.5 million from the Federal Reconstruction Finance Corporation enabled them to lease their own former place of employment and publish the following production schedule: 100 houses a day by September 1947; 125 a day by June 1948; 150 a day by June 1949; 1150 a month by July 1950. In the event the Lustron Corporation went into receivership in June 1950. Its total production of enamelled steel dwellings from January 1947 until closure was 2096 units, and the fastest rate of output ever achieved was six houses a day between March and December 1949.

The Lustron Corporation episode became a scandal. Like the AIROH aluminium prefab in Britain and the Beech Aircraft Corporation financed Wichita house designed by Richard Buckminster Fuller – both of which were also aircraft industry based – it conspicuously failed to transform the house-building industry and do, as Herbert Hoover once predicted, for the working man's home what Henry Ford had done for his car.

Comparatively speaking the AIROH was a great success, with 50 000 built between 1945 and 1948, and comparatively speaking the Wichita was the most advanced, with air-conditioning and two bathrooms – but all three, along with Jean Prouve's prefabs, were total failures at establishing a new industry. Today there may be a dozen AIROHs in Britain and a sprinkling of Lustrons in the southern US. There were only two Wichitas and the one survivor has been heavily modified.

The aerospace branch of the prefabricated home industry, if one might so term it, was the leading edge of the technology of the day. More prosaic dwellings were designed and built using materials ranging from timber to concrete, but all of them shared the ultimate failure of prefabrication in every incarnation save that of the mobile home industry.

Though popular with architects and journalists for the best part of 50 years, the prefabricated dwelling never achieved popular acclaim and is now held in deep execration by the public. An article on the work of visionary prefabricator Buckminster Fuller in a British national newspaper last year drew letters mocking his circular dwellings – 'No room to even hang a dartboard, Fuller has never been in an English pub' – and praise for conventional suburban housing that, 'however badly designed and ornamented since 1920, does at least fulfill the needs of real people'. The letters clearly saw most prefabrication in terms of the heavy concrete systems developed in Germany between the wars and in Britain in the 1960s, and no doubt many of the writers had been educated in prefabricated schools about which they had no complaint, but the message was clear.

The failure of the production-line dwelling is a matter of great importance for architects, if only because so much of the ascendancy once built up by the profession in the industrialized world was intimately bound up with it. Architects today have experienced less difficulty in divesting themselves of the taint of machine production than their public, to whom the matter is still a cause of deep suspicion. It is for this reason that Gilbert Herbert's exhaustively researched *Dream of the Factory-made House* is such a timely book.

Strung loosely around the careers of Walter Gropius and Konrad Wachsmann, Herbert's heavily footnoted narrative does much to clarify to a new generation of readers the reason for the high status of Gropius in Modern Movement history – a status which, lacking reference to his long pursuit of machine-produced building, has waned rapidly since his death in 1969.

Though utterly different in tone and style, Herbert repeats the achievement of Tom Wolfe in *From Bauhaus to our House* in demonstrating the extraordinary cultural and organizational ascendancy that emigre German architects attained in the US during the fourth and fifth decades of the present century. The $37.5 million loaned by the ill-fated Curtiss Wright engineers of the Lustron Corporation was nothing compared with the hundreds of millions poured into prefabrication during World War Two and directed by men who were refugees from their own country – with which the US was at war – and Wachsmann had only contrived to reach the US from Vichy France 3 months before Pearl Harbor.

The foundation of the General Panel Corporation in New York in 1942 for the machine production of war workers' housing placed enormous resources at the disposal of the two German architects, besides which Gropius' chairmanship of the Department of Architecture at Harvard was clearly a matter of small importance. At the time Wachsmann's command of English was, as Herbert records, confined to the inconsequential sentence, 'A thunderstorm refreshes the air'.

In 1941, the last year of peace in the US, prefabrication accounted for 0.5 per cent of the 350 000 new houses completed. By 1943 the percentage had leapt to 16 and the total number of houses completed to nearly 600 000. This was the high-water mark of industrial housing in the terms conceived and developed by Gropius and Wachsmann in the 1920s and 1930s.

General Panel planned post-war production of prefabricated houses at a rate of 10 000 units per annum per factory shift but, as with the Lustron Corporation, such targets proved chimerical and the business was wound up in 1950. At the end a General Panel crew could erect a dwelling in 35 man-hours, but it still could not compete in price with its main competitor, the small builder's timber-framed tract house.

The Dream of the Factory-made House is a deeply researched and authoritative work. Though its two principal characters failed in their quest, the issues they raised about construction and industrial technology cannot be confidently consigned to history.

In Britain today the much publicized issue of the cost of repairing or demolishing our own stock of prefabricated housing only masks the deeper and more alarming question of how low cost dwellings are ever to be provided in the quantities required by the rate of household formation that has accompanied the social fragmentation of all consumer societies. When the myths of the superiority of traditional building and the illusion of maintenance-free construction are finally laid to rest, some global solution to what is already understood to be a new variant of the old housing problem will have to be devised.

At such a time architects might do worse than to revisit the presently despised area of their own history that is called prefabrication. And when they do, they might recall what Konrad Wachsmann wrote in his 1961 book *The Turning Point of Building*: 'Industrialization is not a toy or a passing fashion, it is a building tool which must be mastered'.

MOVING HOUSE

Robert Kronenburg. *Houses in Motion: The Genesis, History and Development of the Portable Building.* Academy Editions, London 1995.

What is the difference between 100 mobile homes and a 3000 m² apartment building? The difference is cultural acceptability. Portable buildings – perhaps a better descriptor in the context of most of the illustrations in this book would have been transportable buildings – have as much history, ingenuity, elegance and future potential as conventional architecture ever mustered, but they are rarely culturally acceptable. Even when they look as though they might be, someone deals from the bottom of the pack – like the wind that destroyed the Future Systems tent in Croydon – and heads start shaking again. Today cultural acceptability decides the issue and architects are in charge of that.

Robert Kronenburg is an author of the number-crunching school, strong on serendipitous research but weak on consistency and narrative drive. In 10 picture-packed chapters he shows a bewildering variety of non-profession-designed artifacts, from tepees and yurts and the barely habitable 19th century Conestoga wagon to the curiously named *Polyconfidence*, a state of the art 800-bed offshore hotel that succours exhausted North Sea oil workers. Despite these riches nothing shakes his confidence that it is architects who should design mobile homes, not the mobile home industry. In this regard the book's introduction by Colin Stansfield Smith is instructive. He writes of the issue of portable buildings being 'ignored, neglected and abused', although what exactly he means by the last is not clear. Perhaps it is he whom Kronenburg echoes when he complains about 'the problem of poorly designed and manufactured portable buildings' that will not go away, but 'moves somewhere else'.

Is this really a problem? Surely what we might term 'the problem of poorly designed permanent buildings' derives almost entirely from their inability to 'move somewhere else'. Ease of disposal is the ultimate value of the (trans)portable and will certainly be seen so as we enter the new century.

TALL STORY

Ada Louise Huxtable. *The Tall Building Artistically Reconsidered.* Pantheon, New York 1984/Trefoil, London 1986.

For an English person, inured to talk of dynamited tower blocks and windswept plazas, leafing through this book is an unnerving experience. It is perhaps facile to say that what we nowadays mean by tall buildings is big buildings, but it is close to the truth. And when we see page after page of gigantic, precise curtain-walled facades rising beyond the capacity of any camera lens to contain their sharp perspective, we know that what has been created is only incidentally a collection of imaginative objects. Their real mainspring has been the production of an enclosed interior landscape, a process whose external drama has been drained by repetition for nearly a century. Louis Sullivan, one of the fathers of modern tall building, knew about this entropy when he wrote in 1923:

> The social significance of the tall building is its most important phase. In and by itself, considered *solus* so to speak, the lofty steel frame makes a powerful appeal to the imagination. Where imagination is absent and its place usurped by timid pedantry the case is hopeless.

In the US, by an effort characteristically beyond the powers of exhausted old Europe, the pretence has been maintained that building tall (or big) is still an artistic problem – something like presenting three views of a human face on a single canvas, as the Cubists tried to do 70 years ago. As a result, critics and architects argue over solutions that not only provide the acres of serviced floorspace that developers need to make the whole project go, but also present curious and complex profiles to philosophize about. While the number of structures exceeding 12 storeys in height steadily increases, a corresponding effort goes into making them all look different – as part of a 'quest' for a skyscraper style appropriate to the centenary of the genre.

As a leading player for more than 20 years, Ada Louise Huxtable, the redoubtable former architecture critic of the *New York Times*, is well aware of the possibilities and limitations of this game. She knows that building high is as much a matter of zoning, tax law, technology and investment as it is a matter of art. But she also knows the truth of Nietzsche's dictum that art is abstract power. One of many similarities between contemporary England and the US is the phenomenal power of art criticism when it locks horns with investment. As she puts it in *The Tall Building Artistically Reconsidered* – the title an act of homage to Louis Sullivan who wrote a similarly named article in1886 – 'One does not expect the larger contextual vision from builders and bankers . . . But one does expect it from architects as part of a responsible design process'. And if they won't deliver it, then they had better look out – so far 'the twentieth century architect's most telling and lasting response to his age is the topless tower of trade'.

So what happens when you reconsider the skyscraper artistically? You get an extremely readable history of tall building that irons out the ideological distortions of Modernist propaganda even as it insists on the authenticity of its genius. Mies van der Rohe's work is bravely identified as the basis of 'the handsomest and most useful set of architecture conventions since the Georgian row houses', while the apotheosis of the International Style is identified in Gordon Bunshaft's 1977 National Commercial Bank in Jeddah. On the way, a large number of eclectic skyscrapers from the first quarter of the century get more recognition and sympathy than they have enjoyed for many years. Indeed, in the later pages, post-Modern and eclectic architecture appear to join hands in the work of Helmut Jahn.

What you do not get is an answer to the problem posed at the beginning. Instead, Huxtable bows out with a series of warnings about hubris, triviality and ground level traffic. Architects, it seems, are not taking a sufficiently serious view of the 200-storey behemoths of the future, and even if they did, the final say-so would not be theirs.

NOT A FAIR COP

Architecture of Incarceration. Foreword by Judge Stephen Tumim, HM Inspector of Prisons. Contributions from Thomas Markus, Leslie Fairweather and Peter Wayne. Academy Group, London 1995.

The strangest thing about prison as form of punishment is that it began in the monasteries of the middle ages. The chroniclers of the monasteries of Cluny and Hirsau both refer to the existence of a *carcer*, a diabolical room accessible only from the top by a ladder and with no door or window. The Cluniacs were at their most influential in the 11th century. By 1206 the idea had spread and the statutes of the Cistercian Order authorized abbeys to have prisons incorporated into their buildings. By the 16th century the concept had been secularized so that most town walls and castle towers incorporated cells in their foundations. At Munster in 1535 one tower alone included two levels of six radial cells for the purpose of imprisonment.

The first modern prison, in the sense of being purposely planned around cells and a large workroom, was the prison of Saint Michael in Rome, which was completed in 1704 to the design of Carlo Fontana. Interestingly enough it was built as a young offenders institution 'for the correction of wayward youth'. It had 20 cells on each of its three floors and each cell had a lavatory, in which sense it was destined to remain advanced for centuries to come.

In the 18th century the designing of prisons became a pastime for intellectuals and reformers, a tendency that reached its apogee in 1791 with the celebrated Panopticon proposal of Jeremy Bentham. This idea for a circular prison building with circumferential cells – each floor designed to be supervised by a single warder at the centre – was in fact part of a general proposal that schools, factories and hospitals could all be designed this way. In practice the anticipated staff economies were not realized in the few prisons built according to Bentham's principle.

By far the most influential prison of the 19th century was the Walnut Street gaol, built in Philadelphia by Quakers in the newly independent US in 1792. The British Inspector of Prisons, William Crawford, was sent to examine it in 1835 and the upshot was a rash of prison building in England starting with Pentonville in 1842. When it was completed, 20 guards could control 400 convicts, which was considered to be a fine achievement – as indeed it was for, when the great

20th century lapse in prison building ended in 1958, the new prisons of the 1960s often required one prison officer for every four convicts. In England this figure reached one prison officer for every two convicts in 1990.

The precise contribution of architecture to the story of modern prisons is what one might reasonably have expected to find in this gaily illustrated book but, to all intents and purposes, it is not there. Despite such innovations as glistening rolls of razor-ribbon wire to replace walls, and 'hotel corridor' plans to replace cell blocks, the dominant influence on the experience of all prisons, even for prison visitors, is established by the regime imposed by the guards, not by the architectural form of the buildings. Indeed the architecture often conceals reality because, in many modern prisons, a deliberate effort is made to obscure 'regime' buildings by means of 'reception' buildings designed by non-specialist architects brought in to provide a dash of colour and an illusion of suburban normality. It is these benign-looking reception buildings that appear to have drawn the attention of the contributors and compilers of *Architecture of Incarceration*, at the expense of a deeper consideration of the relationship between prison and society, or the exceedingly dubious combination of small, autonomous units with restrictive 23-hour a day regimes that is increasingly the norm in developed countries. Today the prison population of the US, a country which has always been devoted to the penal system, stands at over a million and rising. In Europe, Britain leads the way. If this slim but cheerful volume tells us anything it is perhaps that the summary methods employed in Singapore and China have more to recommend them than a feast of architectural photography concealing a bottomless pit of human misery.

ARCHITECTURE THROWS AWAY THE KEY

Architecture & Order: Approaches to Social Space. Edited by Michael Parker Pearson and Colin Richards. Routledge, London 1993.

Thomas A. Markus. *Buildings and Power: Freedom and Control in the Origin of Modern Building Types*. Routledge, London 1993.

It takes only the wail of a police siren to tell us that we are imprisoned by our cities. Ten minutes stopped in a tunnel turns an underground journey into a nightmare. Less drastically we are taught urban imprisonment by the traffic planning of streets, so that whole districts of towns and cities turn into mazes of one-way systems with speed bumps, bollards and culs-de-sac. Even inside our buildings we are trapped. As Karl Marx observed, 'the architect builds the cell in his mind before he constructs it'. So thought the German Modern architect Mies van der Rohe, who said 'Buildings impose order on the space around them'. Perhaps it was the French philosopher Henri Lefebvre who got nearest to the truth when he wrote in *The Production of Space*, 'Monumental buildings mask the will to power and the arbitrariness of power beneath signs and surfaces which claim to express collective will and collective thought'.

Scratch the surface of planning, urban design and architecture and you find a kind of power. In a way buildings represent power above all other things. This power perhaps explains the deep-seated suspicion in which the designers of buildings are held by ordinary people, who live in a world where, as Annie Bartlett ominously observes in her essay in *Architecture and Order*, 'The everyday is getting smaller as the professional gets larger'.

Studying the power embodied in architecture makes a good occult alternative to the bland art-historical litany of styles and periods. For a start it throws up unexpected anthropological data. 'Like some strange race of cultural gastropods', we read in *Architecture and Order*, 'people build homes out of their own essence, shells to shelter their personality. Then these symbolic projections react on their creators, in turn shaping the selves that they are. The envelope thus created is not just a metaphor'. Indeed it is not. It is a lengthy paraphrase of a remark of Winston Churchill's that is never seen in context; 'First we shape our buildings and afterwards our buildings shape us'. But here the authors, two lecturers in archaeology, Mike Parker Pearson and Colin Richards, are using it to describe contemporary suburban life, with its arrays of consumer durables, and its obsession with falling house prices and mortgage traps. As they rightly observe, 'the environment is rarely neutral; it either helps the forces of chaos that make life random and disorganized, or it helps give purpose and direction to one's life'.

Architecture and Order is a collection of essays and papers that range from the interesting to the unreadable, few of them impinge on contemporary life. *Buildings and Power* is a very different kind of book. Not a collection of essays but a epic study by the Emeritus Professor of Building Science at the University of Strathclyde, who endeavours to analyse what he calls the 'social meaning' of all the major new types of building that came into existence with the Industrial Revolution, between 1750 and 1850. Again the idea is to create an alternative taxonomy to that of aesthetic style and architectural celebrity. Thus 19th century hospitals, prisons, asylums, workhouses, libraries and factories are exhaustively, but wittily and readably described, and lugubriously illustrated with original prints. This monochrome presentation gives the book a pleasing uniformity of appearance which is not belied by its contents. Markus deploys massive scholarship in naming, dating and illustrating all the definitive or surviving examples of this or that organizational type of building. His only problem is uniformity of another kind. As his text and his grim pictures make clear, there is a leitmotif of oppression running through virtually all the new building types of the industrial revolution. Hospitals do not escape it, nor do schools, churches (which can be converted into law courts). Perhaps only libraries do. Markus is forced to acknowledge that there is little to choose between architect Sampson Kempthorne's 'Workhouse for 300 paupers' and the architect James Bevans's 'Gaol for 600 prisoners', both of which feature the same cartwheel plan and cellular interior. Nor indeed did things change much whether 'pestilential cholera' was the enemy or the confinement of the insane the object. In the end it is this succession of distinctions without differences that first suggests to the reader that 'power studies' in architecture might turn out to be as arid a discipline as the pursuit of art historical classifications. Grouped together in this way it is clear that all these buildings are oppressive – or at least they were between 1750 and 1850 – and, oddly enough, even the Roman houses illustrated by Clive Knights in *Architecture and Order* make the same point. But this is a reader's view. Markus himself appears to entertain no such doubts. He ends his book by proposing a new kind of 'subversive' architecture based on the power study of buildings that could, by means of skilful design, enable tomorrow's architects to bring about 'shared power relations' in place of the 'oppressive power relations' in which their late 18th and early 19th century clients specialized.

Markus admits that the creation of order is the purpose of all architecture and that this embodies a fatal paradox. It is touching that, at the close of this monumental study, he can only speculate upon simple technical means – easily altered partitioning, user-controlled information systems, occupant-determined shapes and images – that an architect of the future might use to disempower the tyranny of the forces that employ him.

Perhaps the commissioning editors at Routledge thought somewhat along these lines when they began the series 'Approaches to Social Space' to which these two books belong – without alas investigating deeply enough the important question of who was going to buy them.

AN OPEN AND SHUT CASE

Colin Davies. *High-Tech Architecture*. Thames & Hudson, London 1988.

This is a picture book with several hundred fine colour reproductions, line drawings, and black and white photographs. If the reader enjoys looking at beautifully drawn axonometrics of mast-supported structures, stern pictures of Richard Rogers' Lloyd's building against a lowering sky, the rippling fabric of the Mound Stand at Lords cricket ground or black glass boxes deployed in green gardens, then this is the book for them. If on the other hand they are looking for a rip-roaring polemic in favour of advanced technology design in the style of the advertising agency that handles Audi cars – *Vorsprung durch Technik* – then they will be disappointed. *High-Tech Architecture* is a book of works, not words. It is almost as though, in the de-ideologized 1980s, all the best practitioners of industrial-design-for-living-in had reached a corporate decision to advertise their wares without any linking theory at all.

Apart from the project descriptions themselves, the only software in this book is Colin Davies' introduction, a respectably long and interesting essay that the publishers have, for some reason, decided to cram into tiny print and set in two columns across the page so that it is all over virtually before it has begun. Unfortunately deciphering its contents raises more questions than it answers. Searching for the meaning of High-Tech here is singularly unrewarding. For a start, the best Davies can come up with by way of a definition is 'Almost any building designed in the last 20 years by Richard Rogers, Norman Foster, Nicholas Grimshaw, or Michael Hopkins', an amazingly chauvinistic claim, not to say a frivolous answer to a perfectly serious question. And there is worse to come. 'There is something indefinably British about High-Tech', he goes on later, in the best golf club style, 'Perhaps it is nostalgia for the great days when the Empire was serviced and maintained as much by engineers as by industrialists, politicians and generals'.

Perhaps, but in the US the term 'High-Tech' has an equally legitimate etymology dating from the 1970s when it was used to described the style of interior design that incorporated industrial lighting, giant supergraphics across walls and doors, and alloy racing car wheels used as occasional tables. Perversely Davies does illustrate American work (the fine Los Angeles houses of Helmut Schulitz), and he also illustrates German, Dutch and Japanese buildings too, but his narrative belongs securely to the Robert Falcon Scott school of history and genuine overseas precursors to Foster *et al.*, like the pioneering high-tech designers Richard Buckminster Fuller and Charles and Ray Eames, are treated as interlopers at a country house party. Thus the first High-Tech structure cited by Davies is not George Fred Keck's mast-supported ice cream parlor of 1934, but the 1967 Reliance Controls factory built in Swindon by Foster and Rogers, when they worked together as Team 4.

In Davies' view, the history of High-Tech is disappointingly short. Beginning in 1967 it reaches its most advanced incarnation very soon after with the completion of the *Centre Pompidou* in Paris, and achieves its two masterpieces with Rogers' Lloyds and Foster's Hongkong and Shanghai bank. The only substantial American contribution to the history of the genre is to kill it off on January 28th 1986, the day the NASA space shuttle *Challenger* blew up over Cape Kennedy because of a faulty neoprene gasket.

How very unsatisfying.

LARGER THAN LIFE

Chris Wilkinson. *Supersheds: The Architecture of Long-span, Large-volume Buildings*. Butterworth Architecture, Oxford 1991.

There are books to buy on impulse, and there are books to beg, borrow or steal to keep for reference. *Supersheds* is one of the best of the latter category to be published in years. After a decade of superficial picture books devoted to style and fame, in which quality of research and depth of knowledge run a slow third to saturated colour photography, it is deeply satisfying to pore over the mighty structures illustrated here and ponder the ultimate insignificance of the Clore Gallery or Richmond Riverside.

Wilkinson has put together an enviable collection of real long-span, large-volume buildings with the same compulsive fascination as the 1960s' fantasies of the megastructure movement. Starting with Crystal Palace and ending with manifestos from Richard Rogers, Jan Kaplicky, Tony Hunt, Alan Brookes and a (wholly relevant) reprint of part of Sant' Elia's *Messagio*, the author has tracked down extraordinary structures from all over the world and subjected them to clear and useful illustration and description.

There are a thousand fascinations in *Supersheds*. They range from the 'the Model Y Fords of the construction industry', the US Austin Standard Daylight factories produced from 1914; through the career of Albert Kahn, who designed 2000 factories in his lifetime, including an astounding four-fifths of a mile long, air-conditioned, artificially lit, bomber production plant in Texas; on to the 50 000 m² Stansted and the achievements of the High-Tech architects of the present in enclosing more space with less structure than ever before.

If there is a weakness in *Supersheds* it is in Wilkinson's zeal to include any and every non-loadbearing structure that he can under the rubric of his title. Thus such modest structures as the Reliance Controls potentiometer factory become somewhat implausible 'supersheds' too. But this is a minor fault. Buy it. It is worth every penny.

THE LIGHT STUFF

Adriaan Beukers and Ed van Hinte. *Lightness: The Inevitable Renaissance of Minimum Energy Structures*. Uitgeverij 010, Rotterdam 1998.

Did you know that a boomerang is a gyroscope? Do you know what a Mitchell Structure is and what is valuable about it? Do you know the difference between a connoisseur and a collectionneur? Where do people steal natural gas from wells with huge plastic bags? What flying machine is structured by tension alone? What does 'draping prepregs' mean? Have you ever tried sitting in a knotted chair? Are kites really derived from flying tents? In which country have many steel bridge decks been replaced with aluminium ones and why? What stops a bridge engineer from spanning 3.3 km or more with carbon fibre reinforced polymers? How long before cars cease to be made out of steel and buildings start being made out of rigid-rod polymers instead of conventional materials? Who said, 'With composites the designer once more becomes the integrator of form and function'?

The answers to all these questions are to be found in *Lightness: The Inevitable Renaissance of Minimum Energy Structures*, and they all relate to lateral thinking and innovation in the modern world. But not content with breathlessly describing new inventions like a TV presenter reading from an auto cue, the authors of this book explore all sides of innovation. They analyse how it can be encouraged or discouraged. They discover why resistance to it is so strong. They show how this resistance has been overcome in the past in fields ranging from civil engineering to road transport, aviation, marine engineering, architecture and materials technology.

'It will be difficult not to be inspired by what you will read and see', is how the publisher's blurb for *Lightness* winds up and in this case it states nothing more than the truth. *Lightness*, whose two authors originate from the Delft University of Technology in the Netherlands, is a cheaply produced ragbag of absolutely invaluable information. Mistakes? It makes a few, but then again too few to mention. What it gets absolutely right is its polyvalent history of light structures and the evolutionary drive towards efficiency that ensures – as the book's subtitle confidently asserts – that they will always triumph in the end. Taking examples from nature and the vast spread of time from the ancient bow and chariot to modern composites and polymers, as well as boats, planes, cars, bridges and buildings, the authors tantalize with brief narratives and a spectacular collection of images old and new. Clearly intended for students; untouched by glamorous architectural photography; undeterred by a layout artist who drops some captions, makes others read backwards, and sometimes offers no information at all, the book is nonetheless deeply and fundamentally comprehensible. A timely and admirable corrective to coffee table blockbusters of all persuasions.

SOLAR CHALLENGE

Sophia Behling and Stefan Behling. *Sol Power: The Evolution of Solar Architecture*. Prestel, New York 1997.

Perhaps it was the recent news that the world's insurance companies have awoken to the possibility of a global financial crisis that would ruin them and the banks as well unless swift action is taken to avert the kind of claims that could arise as a result of global warming, perhaps it was the culmination of a series of generous EC energy grants. What ever it was, the current view in the West is that environmental issues are intensifying their remorseless march from the distant horizon to centre stage. In the process they are turning their attention to one industry after another – transport, manufacturing, power generation and now construction. The last is an attractive target. In the developed world between 40 and 60 per cent of greenhouse gases emerge from buildings. For this reason alone, in the next 30 years the focus of attention upon building emissions cannot fail to be increasingly intense and restrictive.

Enter the architectural profession, still adrift 20 years after the collapse of the modern movement, having lost an empire and – as far the Dr Kildare-style cruciality enjoyed by the great Modernists is concerned – not yet found a role. But this time the profession scents victory. Whatever else they might be for, buildings are first and foremost about climate control, and climate control in today's buildings is the number one source of thermal pollution. If architects could keep buildings warm or cool without the aid of some gas-guzzling kit that has to be bought from a heating and ventilating manufacturer, cruciality would again be in their grasp.

Step forward Sophia and Stefan Behling, their mentors Sir Norman Foster and Bruno Schindler, and their book *Sol Power*. As its name quaintly implies, this volume is about solar architecture, but that much said, nothing quite prepares a reader for the spectacularly bone-crushing thoroughness of its superb colour photography or the pleasing tone of innocent simplicity and directness with which it explains the whole subject – from the solar system to photosynthesis, and from Mogul architecture to the evolution of industrial technology over 2000 years, the wonder of the geodesic dome and the achievement of man-powered flight. There have been books on solar architecture before, hundreds of them, but none that

I have seen so expansive, so enlightening and so guilelessly convincing as this one. So complete is this survey of the sun's impact on the earth, so enthusiastic its illustration of architecture driven by solar power, and so enthralling any length of time spent leafing through it, that criticism seems superfluous. If there does appear to have been distressingly little proofreading or spell-checking done, and if there is not much by way of a conclusion except an EC resolution or two and a strong hint that the answer lies in the light technology of hang gliders, sail boards and photo-voltaics, no matter. Later editions can sort this out. Meanwhile, anyone who wants a grounding in solar technology and a massive encouragement to 'go solar' in his or her architecture to save the planet should buy it. This book is worth every penny.

DON'T THROW STONES (OR BOMBS)

John Hix. *The Glasshouse*. Phaidon, London 1996.

In dissociating light and atmosphere from the context of the natural overall atmosphere by means of an 'almost ethereal' barrier, ferrovitreous architecture creates a novel condition. Light and atmosphere are now perceived as independent qualities, no longer subject to the rules of the natural world in which they had hitherto manifested themselves. This process is comparable to the experience of pure speed on a railroad, that is, speed perceived as an independent quality because it is divorced from the organic base of horse-power.

So wrote Wolfgang Schivelbusch in his seminal work *The Railway Journey*, published in 1977. It is a quotation missing from *The Glasshouse*, but it is important because it hints at the many pitfalls that have accompanied the architectural fascination for glass construction over the centuries, from the earliest greenhouses and the rise of the concept of achieving automatic climate control by means of a building's envelope. Not that the author is unaware of these pitfalls. He has (inter alia) his own warning quote from Reyner Banham which reads; 'An intelligent commercial glasshouse operator judiciously metering temperature, moisture and carbon dioxide levels . . . has more environmental knowledge at his fingertips than most architects ever learn'.

The story told in this lavish but puritanically overdesigned book is indeed cautionary. Fascinated by glass architecture from his youth – he built a glass dwelling using greenhouse technology at Cambridge in the early 1970s (which does not appear here) and also published a modest book on the subject at that time (which is uncredited) – the mature Hix now sees the field as dominated by little-known 19th century glass house builders who knew more about it than anybody else ever has. Parts of their story almost match the contemporary search for the North West Passage, except that, unlike that classic tale of maritime and Arctic misery, the goal of the old glasshouse builders has still not been fully attained today. Outside the field of horticulture, as the new Foster and Partners' design for a 1200 ft glass tower for the City of London shows us, the concept of perfect transparency remains a kind of holy grail for the achieving architect, however little he or she may be aware of the limitations revealed by its history. In this sense glass architecture may always be a dream repeatedly shattered, as it has been in the 200 years since glasshouses first became synonymous with Modernism, daring, low-cost warmth and technical advance. Just as Joseph Paxton's Crystal Palace was eventually destroyed by fire, so were many other seminal glass structures including its most sincere imitator, the Munich Glass Palace of 1854, and one of its most recent descendants, the polycarbonate glazed 1 acre US Pavilion at Montreal's Expo '67, a spectacularly advanced domical structure that was consumed by flames during refurbishment only 9 years after completion.

In connection with these dramas it is a pity that John Hix's otherwise exhaustive study does not lead to a more impressive conclusion. Instead, after its encyclopedic survey of 19th century glass horticultural and exhibition buildings, it peters out with a scrappy attempt to include at least a picture and a word about more recent examples, some of the most important of which, like Buckminster Fuller's 1954 Saint Louis Climatron, are left out. Perhaps a subsequent edition will remedy this defect. The book deserves it, for it almost inspires the reader to undertake the enterprise of glasshouse building themselves.

LOW ENERGY

Brenda Vale and Robert Vale. *Green Architecture: Design for a Sustainable Future.* Thames & Hudson, London 1991.

According to the London *Sunday Times*, future war will be fought, not by armies of human soldiers, but by thousands of tiny artificial insects which will serve as eyes and ears of the opposing generals and attack by crawling into their opponent's cable ducts and computers and blowing them up.

Of course there is nothing about this in Green Architecture, although the volume is compendious, and does not leave much out from Aristotle and Kafka to compact fluorescent lightbulbs, but the big idea in it strikes the same chord. Leaf through this paperback version of the 1991 original and you realize that architecture too is miniaturizing itself. In future, instead of being a matter of magnificence, with grand plans and vistas, it is going to be a matter of thousands upon thousands of little houses lurking amongst trees, and winning a living from the sun, the wind and the earth.

Let us assume that this will happen. What must be done? The Vales are in no doubt. Build small, build close to, or under the ground. Have a windmill and a tonne of insulation and you are halfway there. The aim is to consume as few resources as possible and make the ones you have consumed available to the builders of the future when you are done. The problem is that buildings like this will owe nothing to the tradition of monumental architecture because, as the authors remind us early on, 'monumental architecture, from its beginnings, is associated with a profligate attitude to resources'. Only a few pieces of great architecture escape and those mostly by special pleading. The Gothic cathedrals, for example, are excused on the technicality that their structure made more efficient use of resources than did the buildings of the Renaissance and because medieval society was not founded on slavery like that of the ancient world. The book proceeds along these lines of 'in' and 'out'. Pretty soon you work out that anything solar cannot fail. Even the solar collectors installed on the roof of the Cary Arboretum in Millbrook, New York, which led to such excessive summer temperatures inside that they were stripped out and replaced by a gas fired central heating system after 1 year, do not fail. According to the Vales, they were removed because they were 'too successful'. In the same way out of town supermarkets (so necessary to sustain suburban life in any civilized society), are deplored as wasteful, while Bedouin tents (not conspicuously prized by air conditioned 4×4-driving Bedouin) are praised for their 'sophisticated performance'. High density housing too – which no one really likes – makes it into the in-list by 'helping to create a sense of community'.

It is a pity that specious argument makes up such a large part of this book. Strip it out and you have a general strategic idea that is fascinating. The problem is that it is not an architectural idea at all.

SEVEN

Cities

A bomber flying over Central London at low altitude, 1951. Source:
© British Crown Copyright/MOD. Reproduced with the permission of
Her Majesty's Stationery Office.

> *The breakdown of the Eastern bloc was the disappear-*
> *ance of a place and the extension of a network.*
> Vilem Flusser 1991

PUT OUT MORE BOLLARDS

Deyan Sudjic. *The 100 Mile City*. Andre Deutsch, London 1992.

There are two politically correct ways to write about cities. The first is in the manner of a latter-day Victorian philanthropist, dwelling on their squalor and communal violence, their collapsing infrastructure, the threat posed by their growing underclass, the economic collapse presaged by their falling property values, the epidemics heralded by their undrinkable water, their poisoned air, gridlocked traffic, uncontrolled crime, deranged street-dwellers, and the thousand individual tragedies of cardboard box living, drugs, poverty and death that pass unnoticed in them every day. The second is far less prolix and gets away with murder. Like the Canary Wharf tower rising above the higgledy piggledy mess of Docklands, it soars above all these grisly details and says instead; 'I LOVE NY'.

As one would expect from the editor of *Blueprint*, the only intellectually respectable English magazine of architecture and design, Deyan Sudjic's book is neither the work of a ragged trousered philanthropist nor easy reading for the average metropolitan booster. Instead it straddles both viewpoints in a bid to master the megalopolitan reality of five 'world cities' that have already broken loose from their old political boundaries and become, for lack of a better phrase, gigantic states of mind. Like a dam-builder, he sets to work to stem and organize the torrential waste of meaning that is urban life. Into the existential black hole of the metropolis he heaves new assemblies; airports and shopping malls, freeways and born-again trams. His chapters contain whole filing cabinets of agreeable and disagreeable urban facts. Everything you ever read in a magazine about London, Paris, New York, Los Angeles or Tokyo is here in *The 100 Mile City*, along with grey, grainy photographs by Phil Sayer that make all the cities look the same, which is of course part of his point. In Sudjic's eyes these 21st century cities 'crackle with energy and are ready to flash over'. They are total cities in the sense that war became total war just before it became practically impossible. Despite the '100 Miles' of the title his cities have no real geographical boundaries; their gates are the doors of airliners; subways and freeways measure their size in travel time; shopping malls are their public arenas; hotels their residential districts; exclusive bars and cafes their most secret places of the heart.

Yet despite his convincing global reach, Sudjic's urban Odyssey seldom bubbles over into actual enthusiasm. The urban view he is most comfortable with is from 40 000 ft. It is as though he knows that, down below on the ground, there is nothing but an untidy gang of politicians, planners, traffic engineers, social workers, journalists, activists, lobbyists, enumerators and arbiters of museums, defenders of art galleries, beggars for cathedrals, concert halls, and architectural competitions who all claim to be running the city. In fact, far from putting the finishing touches to its evolution, they do no more than put out more bollards while the real electricity snaps and crackles beyond distant hills.

In this sense, as a kind of Francis Fukuyama of urban dynamics, Sudjic embraces the post-historical, no longer accountable, out of control, nobody to blame view of the city. Despite all his talk of energy, what he describes in the end is a kind of entropic urban state, half antique, half unborn. Sudjic's great cities have already blurred into one contiguous, lobotomized resting place for restless millions. In later chapters it becomes clear that his view of them is precisely that of the middle management figures he describes seeing at airports all over the world; 'the businessmen, the academics, the consultants, the international flying circus who form part of the perpetually jet-lagged who have become an essential part of the landscape of the modern city'.

Moving unobservably amongst teeming millions, one day on this side of the world, the other on that, these dazed figures are the diametrical opposite to the chauvinistic mayors whose exploits earlier elicited a flicker of qualified admiration. These travelling ciphers with their word processors see only what they want to see. Thus does Sudjic digress on the ethnic structure of Tokyo, then takes a stroll through Southall to wallow in expatriate Asia. He explores public housing on three continents, but also considers Walt Disney's contribution to urbanism in some detail. He has a good word to say for airports, hotels and giant American shopping malls – the new 'public spaces' of our time. He ponders the history of city bids for the Olympic games. Then he hatches three or four pages on the pernicious myth of 'community', which 'has nothing to do with city life', an insight he pursues with zeal, possibly unaware that it comes from a book published in 1974. The same sort of lacunae emerge when he enumerates the sufferings of the Japanese during their 'hardship postings' to London. Sudjic seems not to know that thousands can watch German and Dutch TV in London, and that the deprived expatriate Japanese have their own satellite channel broadcasting from 6 p.m. to midnight.

There are a lot of books about cities around at the moment. There is Mike Davis's *City of Quartz* (about Los Angeles), Saskia Sassens *The Global City* (a significantly larger reach than 100 miles), Joel Garreaus *Edge City* (an interesting study of the boom in peripheral development), and now Richard Rogers and Mark Fishers *A New London*. Sadly what they and *The 100 Mile City* itself really tell us is that it is futile to expect any great insight or real diversity of opinion about great cities. As intellectual subjects they are already ungraspable. As separate entities they have already ceased to exist. Any literary attempt to understand them is doomed to end up with a clutch of jet-lagged authors who not only eat in the same restaurant but fight to be at the same table. If you want a late, late 20th century view, 'I LOVE NY' has to be it.

GREAT CITIES FOUND AND LOST

Spiro Kostof. *The City Assembled: The Elements of Urban Form through History*. Thames & Hudson, London 1993.

There are many ways to look at the phenomenon of urbanism. One is to view the city as one of those hollow, slowly rotating man-made colonies so memorably visualized for NASA 40 years ago: each one a miracle of integrated technology like a Walkman writ large. Another is to ignore all the printed circuitry of modern times and seek instead, in the ancient street plan and among the surviving historic buildings, some trace of an aboriginal settlement, a Saxon village, a medieval town plan or an 18th century etching. The third is to see the city as a powder keg. To rely on the electronic eye of the present, seeing everything through its foreshortened telephoto lens, each vista pregnant with contained energy and incipient conflict, an explosive charge ready to blow.

To attempt to combine all these viewpoints, and to relate them to the world's cities from the dawn of recorded time, is a project so vast that it would only be found credible in the number crunching, book-stacked, picture researched realm of academe. It is a task for a real professor. Someone like Berkeley architectural Historian Spiro Kostof, who has attempted it in two volumes: *The City Shaped: Urban Patterns and Meanings through History*, which dealt with complete cities, and the present work, *The City Assembled*, which deals with the components of which all cities are made up.

Kostof spent 10 years on this project and died before its completion at the age of 55, leaving the two volumes as an encyclopedic memorial to his effort. Both convey a strong sense of a subject so compendious that traces of an attempt at global order defeated by haste and lack of space can be found on every page. Indeed, in the later sections of *The City Assembled*, composed when he already knew that he was dying, few paragraphs escape a massive quota of dashes, slashes, parentheses and footnotes designed to increase their carrying capacity. Kostof strove to make his quotations, insights, pictures and lines of print carry a burden of meaning so heavy that even the crossheads signal ambitions unrealized. 'A Book of Uses', for example, introduces half a dozen pages recording every known use of public open space from Athens in the 2nd century BC to the English New Towns. In the same way a 55-page section entitled 'The Street' begins with a helpless 'The history of the street has yet to be written' and ends with a hopeless 'The street is the burial place of unrehearsed excitement, of the cumulative knowledge of human ways, and the residual benefits of public life'.

Kostof had an immense knowledge of the architecture, planning and history of cities. He knew how many squares, plazas, courts and bridges decorate the world's conurbations, and indeed the precise number of 19th century arcades (280) that can still be found in them. But at least as prominent as his learning was his deep foreboding about the future of the city itself. At the beginning of his first chapter he quotes Giovanni Botero's 16th century definition of the city as 'a congregation of people drawn together to the end they may thereby the better live at their ease in wealth and plenty' and marvels that it includes no reference to plans or buildings. For Botero 'The greatness of a city is not in the largeness of its site or the distance round its walls, but in the multitude and number of its inhabitants and their power'. For Kostof this insight implies the probable doom of the city in the coming century. Take away the wealth and power of its inhabitants, and the fate of the ghost cities of the past, Mycenae, Jerash and Palmyra, looms again in the future.

It is in this vein that Kostof rounds off his mammoth study, with an absorbing survey of urban catastrophes. Rome is consumed by fire in AD 64. Herculaneum is buried by Vesuvius and then rebuilt on top of itself. Established for more than a century, the city of San Miguel de Tucuman in Argentina is moved 100 km north in 1685 after repeated attacks by Indians. London is painstakingly rebuilt after the great fire of 1666, and Lisbon after the earthquake of 1755. Then come the miscellaneous merriments of Modern times. Rotterdam is bombed; burned Lubeck and Nuremberg are traded for bombed Exeter, Bath and York; 8 square miles of Hamburg are destroyed by firestorm; Warsaw is methodically demolished by the retreating Nazis; 16 square miles of Tokyo, and 6 square miles at Hiroshima and Nagasaki are obliterated. Nor does the catalogue of destruction stop at natural and military disasters. Kostof moves on to include the 'rationalization' of Paris by Baron Haussmann; the 'disencumberment' of the ancient monuments of Rome by Mussolini; and the driving of motor roads through the urban fabric of Teheran in the 1930s. Beyond that too is the current enthusiasm for the preservation of large and larger sections of ancient cities as virtual 'time machines'. Kostof saw this too as a danger. He believed that living cities were never still. If they are to survive,

'Process must have the final word. In the end urban truth is in the flow'.

CROW'S FEAT

Robert Sobel. *Trammell Crow, Master Builder: The Story of America's Largest Real Estate Empire*. Wiley, New York 1991.

Not only is Trammell Crow unknown in England, but he has the sort of quintessentially American name that produces smirks or hoots of laughter. Yet Crow was the developer who created modern Dallas, the city that sired TV 'Dallas', the series that taught the 1980s yuppies of the City of London how to cut a deal and gave them Crow-style buildings to do it in.

Born in 1914, Crow never became an architect. For him a building was only part of a deal and he only used his own design talents to save money. The Trammell Crow empire was (and remains, after Crow's recent retirement) an empire of deals. In 1975, when the American economy was deep in the recession caused by the energy crisis and Crow faced what he called 'the crunch' – a threatening landslide of foreclosures that might have overwhelmed his empire of deals – an 'ownership summary chart' of his property interests was drawn up to convince lenders he could survive. The chart is in the book, looking like a spider's web of names with Crow's own at the centre. This bizarre map of the shifting sands of enterprise – plus the information that Crow associates took protective kneepads to their meetings with creditors during 'the crunch' so they could kneel before them – is typical of the strangeness and fascination of this book.

Crow bounced back from 'the crunch', just as he had bounced into property development after service in the procurement division of the navy during the Second World War – which he claimed was 'worth two degrees in business administration'. In the 1950s and 1960s he was filled with a boundless confidence, and put up more buildings than anyone else in America, rapidly becoming several times richer than Donald

Trump could ever have hoped to be. Among other things he is credited with the invention of the modern office/distribution centre. He also had a good line in axioms: 'Work is more fun than fun', 'There is nothing like doing something wrong to teach you how to do it right' and 'I like congestion. It's better than recession'.

LONDON'S BURNING

Blast Effects on Buildings. Edited by G. C. Mays and P. D. Smith. Thomas Telford, London 1995.

This book was specifically written in response to increased professional concern over the problem of protecting buildings from terrorist bomb damage by means of design. The two editors are members of the academic staff at Cranfield University who assembled a number of highly technical essays by experts in the field of explosives so as to define a set of design objectives and lay down guidelines for the attainment of different degrees of blast resistance and the mitigation of blast effects. Despite its modest length the book covers the field fully. It not only discusses the nature of explosions in relation to different building materials and modes of construction, but touches on human behaviour in buildings subjected to blast and outlines a whole range of design measures that will increase the blast resistance of a building likely to suffer terrorist attack. In sum its message is uncompromising: blast-resistance will involve a transformation of the architecture that we know today. Blast-resistant buildings will not only be of simple shapes, lacking exterior surface modelling, but will eschew glass cladding, exterior windows and glass atriums altogether. In effect the entire repertoire of traditional and modern details will either cease to be used, or will disappear behind a smooth-skinned envelope without reveals or recesses where explosive devices could be concealed. Cladding panels will be easily replaceable for repair. Finally, access, exit and parking regimes for the occupants of such buildings will be strictly controlled.

Where *Blast Effects on Buildings* falls short is in describing
the circumstances which led to the decision to contemplate
changes in building design that not even World War Two
produced. This is a pity, for there is an enthralling story of
massive damage and cost to be told in linking the politics of
terrorism in the UK with the slow evolution of a static defence
through design. Its scale was first hinted at 12 months before
the IRA ceasefire of 1994, when an opposition Labour MP,
Mr Martin Redmond, asked a question in parliament that
brought forth cries of 'shame', 'swine' and 'disgrace' from the
government benches. His question was a very simple one. He
asked the Home Secretary to state the cost, location by location, of bomb-proofing government and civil service premises
throughout England and Wales.

The reason Mr Redmond's question provoked such rage
was because it touched upon the guilty secret of the end of the
'war against terrorism' that successive British governments
waged from 1969, when the recent troubles in Northern
Ireland broke out, until the ceasefire. The guilty secret was
that the cost of fighting the IRA in mainland Britain was what
finally brought John Major's government to the conference
table with the IRA. At an estimated £3.5 billion a year the
direct cost of policing Northern Ireland might have been bear-
able: what was wholly unacceptable was the damage terrorist
attack did to the mainland economy, notably to the £20 billion in invisible earnings of the 524 banks and 8500 financial
firms in the square mile of the City of London. From
November 1971, when a bomb shattered the revolving
restaurant at the top of the 660 ft British Telecom Tower – a
facility that has never since reopened its doors to the public –
to the two huge bombs that devastated the streets around the
Bank of England in April 1992 and April 1993, it was the economic damage inflicted by bombing, and the threat of bombing, that won the war for the Irish Republicans.

Both the big City bombs were body blows to the British
economy. The first initiated over £700 million in insurance
claims and the second over £1 billion. Landmark financial services buildings like the NatWest Tower, the Stock Exchange,
the Baltic Exchange, the Commercial Union and a dozen other

major structures were blitzed and took years to repair. The second City bomb actually went off during a meeting of the council of the European Bank of Reconstruction and Development, an event which led, within a week, to direct warnings to the government from several foreign banks that, unless London could be made safe, they would relocate to Brussels, Paris or Frankfurt.

The Corporation's response was a massive and crippling security clamp-down. In July 1993, after a third IRA bomb had been defused minutes before it was scheduled to go off at the foot of the 850 ft Canary Wharf Tower in London's Docklands, a makeshift 'Berlin Wall' of concrete and plastic blocks manned by armed policemen was erected across all vehicular entry points into the City of London. Later still, after the diversionary IRA mortar attack on Heathrow Airport in March 1994 – an event timed to coincide with the annual renewal of the civil rights-limiting Prevention of Terrorism Act by parliament – Metropolitan police chief Paul Condon announced that armed policemen would have to patrol the capital indefinitely. After the 1992 Baltic Exchange bomb in the City, 24-hour surveillance cameras had already been installed throughout the financial district.

Nor were road blocks, security measures and armed policemen enough. By the end of 1993 the City of London had decided to embark on a costly rebuilding programme that was designed to involve the very architecture of London in a massive system of anti-terrorist defences. This was the measure that Mr Redmond's parliamentary question referred to: a measure that soon became the hottest potato in architecture, planning and politics in London. The major players in the financial sector were not content with the 'Berlin Wall' they had erected around themselves. They demanded yet more security. They began to convert the underground carports of their financial services buildings into £1 million bomb shelters. The half-tonne Baltic Exchange bomb of 1992 and the one tonne Bishopsgate bomb that went off in 1993 succeeded where Hitler's bombers had failed. They brought the City to its knees and changed the course of urban history.

In the event the ceasefire put a stop to this programme almost as soon as it has begun. After the barricading of Downing Street came the nocturnal barricading of the foreign banks and newspaper offices at Canary Wharf. Next in line to be built was a 'fortress city' around the government offices in Whitehall. Next was to come a fourth exclusion zone around the exclusive shopping areas of Knightsbridge and Bond Street, followed by others designed to protect the Royal Parks and Palaces. In this way London was to have come to resemble Belfast, the capital of Northern Ireland, where the urbanism of terror began a quarter of a century ago. This much might have given an added dimension to *Blast Effects on Buildings*.

LOS ANGELES, LOST FOR WORDS

Mike Davis. *City of Quartz: Excavating the Future in Los Angeles.* Verso, London 1990.

The way I remember Los Angeles it was like living in one of those hollow, slowly rotating man-made colonies visualized by artist Fred Wolff for Martin Caidin's 'Worlds in Space'. I particularly remember experiencing this sense of circularity whenever I scaled some eminence to look down on it. Loyola Marymount University, the Griffiths Observatory, the mountains north and East: wherever you went the result was always like the space colony, more and more of the same thing curving upwards and outwards around you so that, but for the blurring effect of the smog and sunlight, you could have seen it meet miles over your head in a seamless tube – with you and 12 million others humming quietly on the inside.

This was clearly an illusion. As unravelled by the Mike Davis school of Los Angeles scholarship, the City of Quartz is not integrated at all and far from meeting over your head it all but comes apart beneath your feet. Nowadays its identity is only an opinion, while its reality consists largely of reefs of older utopian settlements encrusted with new walled enclaves and public housing projects and shopping centres modelled on Jeremy Bentham's Panopticon prison, with sub-stations of the Los Angeles Police Force at the eye of every radiating mall. The space colony is actually a fragmented erewhon for the proper intellectual definition of which a large prize is perpetually on offer.

It is attempts to define Los Angeles, followed by sociological vignettes and narratives of crimes, or booms, or industries that bring the definitions down in flames, that make up the weight of this extraordinarily long book. Davis has a library of Los Angeles knowledge of Brobdignagian proportions and is able to quote from sources going forward to the initiative banning gasoline powered cars by the year 2010, back to the 1880s, or anywhere in between, with the words of people who walked to Los Angeles from Ohio, hitchhiked there from Bolivia or were imported regardless of expense to manage cultural events like the 1987 Los Angeles Festival – the director of which, one Peter Sellars, he quotes pontificating Stephen Bayley-style; 'There is certainly a sense of genuine immaturity about Los Angeles, but I don't think that is entirely to be deplored – I think it is interesting'. A curiously inadequate word to use of a city the size of Ireland, with a higher gross product than the subcontinent of India and a projected population of 18 million in 20 years time.

Needless to say Davis does not share the 1987 Festival view of Los Angeles as immature and interesting. He has a bigger grasp, not least of its physical size, extending from the western commuter horizon of Ventura County, north into the real estate mirage of Antelope Valley (called Death Valley as late as 1973 then cynically stocked with a few antelopes later as an aid to sales and now one of those places where 'developers don't just grow homes in the desert . . . they clear, grade and pave, hook up some pipes to the local artificial river . . . build a security wall and plug in the "product"'), then east into the shrivelled tailings of the Coachella Valley, south east into Riverside and then due south round the engulfed port of Long Beach to Orange County and eventually San Diego.

Just as he knows Los Angeles geography, Davis knows Los Angeles history too: pioneering, cultural, entrepreneurial, artistic, military-industrial, intellectual, criminal, racial, economic, everything from Miller's Model Farms, through the Young People's Socialist League, to Henry J. Kaiser, 'Rosie the Riveter' and the Rouse Corporation. Oh the humanity of it! It is all here from Nathanael West to 'Blade Runner', all at intimidating length and with that terrifying Noah's Ark completeness that American intellectuals require of their tours d'horizon.

To help articulate the intellectual part of this gargantuan feast Davis has divided its performers into three groups: boosters, people he calls 'noirs' and 'mercenaries'. The boosters are the natives or immigrants who more or less think that Los Angeles is great – the city of the second chance, in a popular middle-aged phrase. The 'noirs' are natives or immigrants who say it is a dystopic nightmare heading for a hell of drugs and violence – if it is not already there. The 'mercenaries' are megaphone media people bought in by the boosters to talk so loud that they can make the world count the art galleries and not the gang killings. These people are el cheapo versions of the flacks and hacks regularly bussed into Glasgow to chant that it really is a great city and not just the spavined envious sharp end of a bottle. Of course the Los Angeles mercenaries get paid a great deal more for their soothsaying than the Scots mercenaries. Take Michael Sorkin for instance: 'LA is probably the most mediated town in America, nearly unviewable save through the fictive scrim of its mythologizers'. ($20 000 please.)

I had a lot of trouble figuring out just what Davis did believe in until I struck quartz (as it were) about page 80 of this book. At that point the debunked cavalcade of celebs and celebrated victims suddenly gave way to some characters I recognized. Here came the professors from SAUP, the School of Architecture and Urban Planning at UCLA, amongst whom I spent the academic year of 1979/80. I remember the planning school in particular, as a place chronically denuded of students except for Iranian refugees and enthusiasts for child care, parenting and 'what would a feminist city be like?' chautauquas (as they called their group agreement sessions). One afternoon I arrived to take my own class and heard the sound of singing echoing through the corridors. It was the planning professors rehearsing union songs for a Labor Day march.

To my surprise it is one of these same singing professors who heads Davis's list of 'brave beginnings'. Step forward Ed Soja with an essay entitled 'It All Comes Together in Los Angeles' which, sociological guide-book style, has this to say of the city:

> One can find in Los Angeles not only the high technology industrial complexes of the Silicon Valley and the erratic sunbelt economy of Houston, but also the far-reaching industrial decline and bankrupt urban neighbourhoods of rustbelt Detroit or Cleveland. There is a Boston in Los Angeles, a lower Manhattan and a South Bronx, a Sao Paulo and a Singapore. There may be no other comparable urban region which presents so vividly such a composite assemblage and articulation of urban restructuring processes. Los Angeles seems to be conjugating the recent history of capitalist urbanization in virtually all its inflectional forms.

Or as the old *News of the World* used to put it; 'All Human Life is There'. And, as Peter Sellars (no relation, I'm sure), might have been tempted to add; 'There is certainly a sense of genuine immaturity about it, but I don't think that is entirely to be deplored'.

MODEST UTOPIANS

Sim Van der Ryn and Peter Calthorpe. *Sustainable Communities: A New Design Synthesis for Cities, Suburbs and Towns*. Sierra Club, San Francisco 1986.

Some years ago the French sociologist Henri Lefebvre spoke at a symposium at the New York Museum of Modern Art on the subject of planning the university of the future. As is invariably the case on such occasions, discussion rapidly diffused to encompass the future of the world and what to do about it, and Lefebvre's contribution was memorably cynical. 'There is nothing wrong with the world at all', he said. 'It is like a ship sailing across the ocean of the universe: the only problem is that the ship is on fire and there is no communication between the bridge and the engine room.'

When these words were translated into English there was some nervous laughter but little direct response. After all, planners always behave as though they are on the bridge with the captain while the engine room of the economy patiently waits for orders. Any suggestion that they might only be passengers – and worse still that there might be maniacs in the engine room who leave the phone off the hook while the steam pressure goes into the red zone – tends to affect them the way a hand with four aces affects a poker school. Thus it is with *Sustainable Communities*, which is not a book with a beginning a middle and an end, but a seamless collection of didactic essays in the modern manner.

In reality of course everything is worse even than Lefebvre described it. Not only is the captain a powerless figurehead who only appears to direct the ship, but the planners are psychopathic passengers who impersonate ship's officers for reasons of their own. Worse still, the advice they give to the captain consists of nothing more than what they read in *Scientific American* last week or saw on TV the night before. Even the engineers who really make things go have no idea what they did yesterday or what they will do tomorrow because they keep no records and never go on deck. Periodically they find to their amazement that they have been carrying out some master plan – Cite Industrielle, Radiant City, Garden City, Broadacre City, Milton Keynes – when all the time they thought they were just bending the rules and making the ship go faster. That is what we call history. Most planners of repute have enjoyed the flush of pride that comes with being consulted by the UN or invited to join the Governor's housing task force. Nothing much ever comes of it, but it looks good on the CV. That is when they tell the engineers what they have been doing: it is the part they play in history.

Sustainable Communities dates from the big scare about energy that followed the 1973 oil embargo. For the first time since 1942 the engineers finally got worried about the direction of the ship because there was (temporarily) no gas for their cars. Lots of planners got invited to join the Governor's task force at that time. In their way they made the most of it, because it was then that the idea of some kind of harmonious coexistence of high technology and the natural world by way of earth berms, solar cells and bicycles finally made its way onto the engine room agenda. You may recall Jimmy Carter and his White House solar water heaters, the ones they removed earlier this year. In *Sustainable Communities* Sim Van der Ryn and Peter Calthorpe have put the entire theory together; the result is like a 5-year-old chart laid before the captain as the ship approaches an area of tricky shoals.

The sustainable economy is perhaps the only idea to have survived into the folklore of late 20th century government intact from that heady time of turned down thermostats and million dollar solar houses. Each of the essays in the book – bar the last, which is an admirable illustrated primer on 20th century New Towns thinking by Peter Calthorpe, and a more than usually restrained piece on the golden future of alternative transportation systems by Fred A. Reid – is steeped in the fulsome optimism of the post industrial pre-AIDS era. David Katz's evocation of a 'sustainable city' sums it up best:

> Imagine a New York or Los Angeles, the city a patchwork of fields intermixed with garden-roofed office towers and apartment buildings, bisected by tree-lined corridors. The sun glistens on the varied panes of the greenhouses and growing frames that are part of the buildings and malls of the city. A business executive, refreshed by the scented, cooling breeze coming from the quilted fields, pauses for a moment beneath a fruit tree before entering her workplace . . .

'Sounds good, doesn't it?', continues Katz. Well yes, I suppose it does, especially the delayed 'her' instead of the 'him' that you are expecting, but there is also a wish-fulfilling tone here borrowed from the world of advertising that bodes ill. There is more of it in 'Design as if People Mattered', a contribution by Clare Cooper Marcus, who has a way with simple ideas; 'I mean by family anything that considers itself a family' is one of them (one wonders if this includes Charles Manson's 'Family'?); 'By 1990, 80 per cent of all preschool children will be in day care' is another; 'Stop the child murders' is a third. Is there a connection between children in day care and child murders, or is it all a matter of housing layouts? Cooper Marcus appears not to know much about property values, she thinks design counts.

Then there is the theoretical core of the book, 'The Mass and Information Economy' by Paul Hawken. I must admit I was very impressed with the opening paragraphs – 'Current economic problems are no more a sign of failure than adolescence is a sign of the failure of childhood' – but later the old irreconcilable contradictions come flooding back in. 'While the United States does not want to go back to a labor-intensive agriculture to save energy', intones Hawken threateningly, 'Our only hope of supplying sufficient amounts of food for ourselves and others is to have more people on the land working ever more productively'. Why invoke the example of the Chinese peasant unless that is what you mean?

When you get down to it even the case studies in the book, where the authors imply that the whole thing has been done already, turn out to be fakes. Take the compact Chino Hills development that claims a one-third energy saving over nearby 'sprawl' suburbs by minimizing auto trips, energy-conserving design, and rigorous site planning and building standards. In the last paragraph of a rapturous description it is revealed that half the claimed energy saving is derived from a theoretical extrapolation of the reduction in auto trips. It makes one wonder what the direct energy cost of the rest was.

The problem with *Sustainable Communities* is contained in Hawken's essay where he builds up a watertight case for the collapse of Western civilization through pollution and resource exhaustion, then abandons it in favour of a happy ending. Or maybe that was the captain's idea.

NEW AGE URBANISM

Richard Rogers. *Cities for a Small Planet.* Edited by Philip Gumuchdjian. Faber & Faber, London 1997.

Like the Reith Lectures of 1995 from which it was developed, this book deals with a paradox: cities are abominable places that are destroying the planet, but they are also vibrant, convivial, life-enhancing centres of civilization. In a switchback series of optimistic and pessimistic passages that is sustained for the full length of the book, the author tries to produce a synthesis from these two positions, starting out in pessimistic vein but invariably ending up firmly on the optimistic side. The book thus takes on the character of a Jeckyll and Hyde battle between extremes that is never properly resolved.

According to the opening chapter, cities are responsible for accelerating the rate of terrestrial pollution and erosion; destroying our ecosystem; threatening humankind's survival; generating the majority of greenhouse gases; undermining the ecological balance of the planet; being built at a phenomenal rate and density with little thought for future environmental or social impact; producing disastrous social instability that is further driving environmental decline; creating ecological and social problems that dominate the human scene; increasingly polarizing society into segregated communities, and becoming little more than no-man's lands for scurrying pedestrians or sealed private cars (specifically those with tinted windows and central locking) that 'prevent people from participating in street life'.

This sounds bad but, in the next chapter, Dr Jeckyl makes his appearance and prises Mr Hyde's fingers from the word processor. The picture immediately brightens. To turn city life around, we learn, it is only necessary to 'demand fundamental changes in human behaviour, the practice of government, commerce, architecture and city planning'. Nowhere is it acknowledged that this is rather a tall order. Instead the alleged means of bringing it about are painstakingly broken down into bite-size morsels, like the step by step instructions for personal salvation offered by the Church of Scientology. Indeed the thoughts of Richard Rogers and the formidable editing skills of Philip Gumuchdjian, invisibly joined as they are here, often rise to a soothingly incantatory tone reminiscent of the late L. Ron Hubbard.

When strolling through Europe's great public spaces – the covered Galleria in Milan, the Ramblas in Barcelona, the parks of London or the everyday public spaces of markets and local neighbourhoods – Richard Rogers tells us that he 'feels part of the community of the city'. This is convincing, for he writes easily, not only of London and Paris, but of Shanghai, Marrakesh, Venice, Rotterdam, Ciritiba in Brazil and other places known to even fewer people. Subtly, in his emollient flow of words, he contrives to move architecture up from fourth to first in the hit-list of 'fundamental changes' – and not just architecture, to judge by the vast majority of the illustrations, the architecture of the Richard Rogers Partnership in particular. To be sure there are occasional bleak moments when Mr Hyde reasserts himself – he obviously got to work on the city government of Shanghai and persuaded them to build roads for cars instead of accepting Dr Jeckyll's enlightened ped-o-cycle city plan – but in general the answer seems to be the eternal sustainable city of the rich with its sunshine, tourists, sidewalk cafes, parks, rivers, great architecture, great restaurants, conviviality, vibrance and the unspecified 'street life' that Mr Rogers finds most acceptable. As Charles Jencks once advised in relation to another matter: whenever faced with two extremes, always pick a third. Perhaps the kindest thing one can say about *Cities for a Small Planet* is that its author follows this counsel to the letter.

An example from the third chapter makes this clear. It concerns two different concepts of housing. The first is a system of prefabricated tower blocks assembled by crane, based on a single residential 'box' the size of a standard shipping container. It was developed by the Richard Rogers Partnership for a South Korean client in 1991. The second, by an architect named Shigeru Ban in Kobe, Japan, is a self-build emergency housing system capable of withstanding hurricane force winds that is made of rolled tubes of waste paper and planks of wood with beer crate foundations. Here are two invidious choices. In Taiwan ex-convict taxi drivers live in appalling squalor in shipping containers dumped under bridges; in London people sleep in cardboard boxes in the street. How long are we expected to believe that this 'emergency housing' made from paper tubes will last?

Richard Rogers neatly sidesteps all this disagreeableness. 'Both these concepts encourage a vibrant society and reinforce the social dimension of environmental sustainability', he writes, moving quickly on. With the aid of the words 'vibrant', 'social', 'environmental' and 'sustainable', all in the same sentence, he comes smiling through.

NO AUTOMOBILE EVER BOUGHT A THING

Richard Longstreth. *City Centre to Regional Mall: Architecture, the Automobile and Retailing in Los Angeles 1920–1950.* MIT Press, Cambridge, MA 1997.

This is a dense, profound, monochrome and encyclopaedic study (in all save its curiously deficient index) of a subject that seems at first arcane, but soon emerges as central to the whole issue of urban development and sustainable growth in the future. Longstreth's narrative begins with accommodation of the motor car into the planning of the American city, moves on to the early years of the disurbanization of retail in the 1930s and 1940s, and concludes with the post-World War Two development of the small out of town shopping malls that are instantly recognizable as the ancestors of the giants still being built today. Thus in his chosen space of only 30 years (although the indefatigable Longstreth also includes much material on earlier and later retail designs), he succeeds in explaining how the most advanced society on earth created the infrastructure of mass consumption that the rest of the world has adopted today.

Among the many surprises thrown up by this study of over 200 shopping centres, many, if not most, no longer in existence, is the evidence it offers of the extent to which urban planning in the US had successfully reconciled itself to the invasion of the automobile as early as the mid-1920s. Given the drastic allocation of whole urban blocks for parking, and the profusion of basement, and seven and eight storey overground parking garages alongside or surmounted by department stores – all of which existed in the US as early as 1924 – and given the survival in business of many city centre department stores up to the present day (even in Los Angeles, the paradigm of automotive decentralization), it is evident that the emergence of out of town shopping centres was a more complex phenomenon than might have been thought. As the planner Victor Gruen put it; 'No automobile, not even a Cadillac, ever bought a thing'. So in the US the suburbanization of shopping was not so much driven by car ownership as gambled upon it. Parking was important, but the chainstore retailers who first made the move to the suburbs and beyond took their counter-commuting chance in search of profits – they could not prosper in the downtown areas because city centre retail floorspace was sewn up by cartels of the older major department stores.

In architectural terms there is little that looks revolutionary to us today in Longstreth's extensive cast of shopping projects. Throughout his period, as is the way with business ideas, anything successful was copied exactly with innovation seen as an unnecessary risk. The very few totally innovative schemes owe everything to extraordinary circumstances, as for instance the influential 1942 plan for a shopping centre to serve the hastily built defence housing for the World War Two bomber plant at Willow Run, near Detroit, by Eero Saarinen.

Perhaps the biggest lesson in this book dawns on the reader slowly. If the road from inner city to out of town retail was as incrementally ponderous as Longstreth shows it to have been, the route back to urban centrality, public transport and reduced pollution seems almost certainly unattainable. Scanning the aerial views of shopping centres here – all of them much smaller and more suburban than the projects that followed them – reminds one of the famous Irish answer to an appeal for directions; 'If I was going there, I wouldn't start from here'.

EIGHT

TV Programmes

Source: Author.

The fundamental event of the Modern Age has been the conquest of the world as a picture.

Martin Heidegger 1962

PATERNOSTER PRANKS

Signals: Let the People Choose. Channel 4,
Wednesday 28 March 1990.

It must be 20 years since Roger Graef first started filming face-to-face conflict and cooling it down into an art form. At first it was local government but now, as befits the times, it is the environment. Just as Lenin believed that communism equalled the soviets plus electrification, so Graef has come to believe that participation equals popular opinion plus television. For him it has become a crusade. He knows his Oliver Wendell Holmes too: the camera is a mirror with a memory. As a result, the hidden agenda for the discussions that make up most of 'Let the People Choose', was the idea that 'ordinary people' really might have a bigger say in planning decisions, if only they went on television to get it.

But Graef's arena this time was the already punch-drunk Paternoster development and, on this showing, his proposition seemed considerably doubtful. The programme was built up on the back of a massive market research operation that had determined what random and regular users of the area thought.

The unfolding of public opinion showed that while two people had stumbled upon once-radical architectural ideas – one wanted a glass dome over Saint Paul's (*viz.* Richard Buckminster Fuller 1962) and another wanted the cathedral surrounded by parkland (*viz.* the MARS plan 1944) – most seemed to have safely impractical aims for the site. With the proviso that there should be no offices, they would have settled for a jolly mixture of low-rent housing, cafes, shops and local amenities.

Graef then put these demands to Peter Rees, chief planning officer for the City of London. To at least one viewer's amazement, Rees replied: 'I think that all squares with our plans very well'. The other members of the panel, from Trevor Osborne of the British Property Federation to Pasternoster brief-writer Frank Duffy (who had been to Sweden and seen the future and it worked) enthused too. Only Terry Farrell, to his credit, doubted that such a project could be put into effect straight away.

Luckily, the question of who was really being sensible here was also settled by the public. At one point, Graef admitted that none of those consulted actually believed their opinions would have any affect at all. How shrewd of them.

CAPTURING ARCHITECTURE

Skyscraper. A five-part weekly series on Channel 4 starting on Sunday November 26th 1989.

Karl Sabbagh. *Skyscraper: The Making of a Building.* Macmillan (in association with Channel 4), New York. 1989.

The book is good, but the TV series is an epic not to be missed. This well-synchronized combined release is one that should be watched or read by anybody who wants to know how monster buildings are built, and how architecture really fits into the social, political and economic context of development in the late 20th century. Though broken up into episodes by the exigencies of TV, and lacking any hero save the building itself, 'Skyscraper' captures the irresistible momentum, pride and excitement that a building project generates among all those taking part in it. 'Skyscraper' shows the viewer, if not perhaps the reader – for the book is little more than a transcript of the narrators voice – exactly why construction is not just an expensive way of wrecking the environment, best carried out apologetically if at all. 'Skyscraper' shows the construction of a giant building for what it really is, a vast, complex and awe-inspiring creative task.

To make this extraordinary record Karl Sabbagh, producer of Jonathan Miller's 'The Body in Question' for the BBC and the anthropological series 'Strangers Abroad' for Central, spent 4 years filming the gestation and completion of the million square foot, 47-storey Manhattan skyscraper 'Worldwide Plaza'. Even now, cut down to manageable length, his film still finds room for the history of the site; the plot ratio wheeler-dealing that gave the developer what he wanted; the public participation meetings (where some soon-to-be decanted tenants wondered aloud why they needed new bathrooms when they had been given new bathrooms as recently as 1938); the design of the monster brick-clad post-Modern building itself by David Childs of SOM; the worldwide chain of sub-contracting that fed its construction; the weekend village lives of the Iroquois ironworkers who built the towering steel frame (with I-beam steel crosses marking the graves of those who fell to their deaths); the truckdrivers, dispatchers, expediters, managers, millionaires, right down to the advertising men who worried about the neighbourhood when they leased 13 floors straight off the drawing board.

In addition to its enthralling narrative there are fascinating historical references in 'Skyscraper'. Not only was the site once the home of world heavyweight title fights, but Childs, architect of 'Worldwide Plaza', the scion of Modern skyscraper builders Skidmore Owings and Merrill, is shown in the full flood of tantric historicism insisting on brick facings 700 ft up and an elliptical arcade around the base of the building when the steelwork has already been designed. Even the developer has a past. Bill Zeckendorf Jr is the son of William Zeckendorf, the once bankrupted New York developer who bought Frank Lloyd Wright's Robie House to save it from demolition in 1959.

For years there has been a crying need for a television approach to architecture with more realism than Christopher Martin/HRH productions; more technical grasp than your average opinionated young fogey discriminating between 'tinny' and 'woody'; and more driving narrative than Peter Adam's completed buildings in bright sunshine with the voice of Andrew Sachs saying how good they all are. 'Skyscraper', written and produced in book and video form by Sabbagh himself, has all these things and more. Watch it.

Bibliography

A Critic Writes: Essays by Reyner Banham. Selected by Mary Banham, Paul Barker, Sutherland Lyall and Cedric Price. Foreword by Peter Hall. University of California Press, San Francisco 1997.

Adam, Peter. *The Arts of the Third Reich*. Thames & Hudson, London 1990.

Alexander, Christopher. *A City is not a Tree*. University of California at Berkeley, San Francisco 1966.

Allan, John. *Berthold Lubetkin*. RIBA, London 1992.

Alofsin, Anthony. *Frank Lloyd Wright the Lost Years 1910–1922: A Study of Influence*. University of Chicago Press, Chicago 1993.

Appleyard, Bryan. *Richard Rogers, A Biography*. Faber & Faber, London 1986.

Architectural Competitions 1792–1949 (Volume I) and 1950–today (Volume II). Edited by Cees de Jong and Erik Mattie. Benedikt Taschen, Cologne 1995.

Architecture of Incarceration. Foreword by Judge Stephen Tumim, HM Inspector of Prisons. Academy Group, London 1995.

Architecture & Order: Approaches to Social Space. Edited by Michael Parker Pearson and Colin Richards. Routledge, London 1993.

Banham, Reyner P. *Theory and Design in the First Machine Age*. Architectural Press, London 1960.

Banham, Reyner P. *Design by Choice*. Academy Editions, London 1981.

Banham, Reyner P. *The Architecture of the Well-tempered Environment*. Architectural Press, London 1969.

Bartos, Adam and Christopher Hitchens. *International Territory: The United Nations 1945–95*. Verso, London 1994.

Behling, Sophia and Stefan Behling. *Sol Power: The Evolution of Solar Architecture*. Prestel, New York 1997.

Benevolo, Leonardo. *The Origins of Town Planning*. Routledge & Kegan Paul, London 1967 (first published as *Le Origini dell Urbanistica Moderna*. Editori Laterza, Bari 1963).

Bertram, Anthony. *The House: A Machine for Living In*. A & C Black, London 1935.

Bertram, Anthony. *Design*. Pelican, London 1938.

Beukers, Adriaan and Ed van Hinte. *Lightness: The Inevitable Renaissance of Minimum Energy Structures*. Uitgeverij 010, Rotterdam 1998.

Blake, Peter. *The Master Builders*. Gollancz, London 1960.

Blast Effects on Buildings. Edited by G. C. Mays and P. D. Smith. Thomas Telford, London 1995.

Boudon, Philippe. *Lived in Architecture: Le Corbusier's Pessac Revisited*. Dunod, Paris 1969/Lund Humphries, London 1972.

Boudon, Philippe. *Pessac de Le Corbusier: 1927–1967: Etude Socio-architecturale. Collection Aspects de l'Urbanisme*. Dunod, Paris 1969.

Boyce, Robert. *Keck and Keck*. Princeton Architectural Press, New York 1993.

Brett, Lionel. *Ourselves Unknown: An Autobiography*. Gollancz, London 1985.

Buderath, Bernard. *Peter Behrens: Umbautes Licht*. Prestel Verlag, Frankfurt 1990.

Burkle, J. Christopher. *Hans Scharoun*. Artemis, London 1993.

Cacciari, Massimo. *Architecture and Nihilism: On the Philosophy of Modern Architecture*. Yale University Press, New Haven, CT 1993.

Cherry, Gordon E. and Penny Leith. *Holford: A Study in Architecture, Planning and Civic Design*. Mansell, London 1986.

Christo: The Reichstag and Urban Projects. Edited by Jacob Baal-Teshuva. Prestel, London 1993.

Cities of Artificial Excavation: The Work of Peter Eisenman 1978–1988. Edited by Jean-Francois Bedard. Canadian Centre for Architecture/Rizzoli International Publications, New York 1995.

Clough, Rosa. *Futurism: The Story of a Modern Art Movement*. Praeger, New York 1961.

Cohen, Jean-Louis. *Scenes of the World to Come: European Architecture and the American Challenge 1893–1960*. Canadian Centre for Architecture/Flammarion, London 1995.

Collins, George. *Antonio Gaudi*. George Braziller, New York 1960.

Conrads, Ulrich and Hans Sperlich. *Fantastic Architecture*. Verlag Gerd Hatje, Stuttgart 1960.

Construction Disasters: Design Failures, Causes and Prevention. Edited by Steven Ross. McGraw-Hill, New York 1984.

Cook, Peter. *Architecture: Action and Plan*. Studio Vista, London 1967.

Cooke, Philip. *Back to the Future: Modernity, Postmodernity and Locality*. Unwin Hyman, London 1990.

Le Corbusier. *Towards a New Architecture*. Translated and with an introduction by Frederick Etchells. Architectural Press, London 1927 (first published by Georges Cres, Paris 1923).

Le Corbusier. *Concerning Town Planning*. Architectural Press, London 1948 (first published by Editions Bourrelier et Cie, Paris 1946).

Le Corbusier. *The City of Tomorrow*. Translated and with an introduction by Frederick Etchells. Architectural Press, London 1929.

Le Corbusier. *The Decorative Art of Today*. Translated and with an introduction by James Dunnett. Architectural Press, London 1987.

Crinson, Mark and Jules Lubbock. *Architecture – Art or Profession? Three Hundred Years of Architectural Education in Britain*. Manchester University Press, Manchester 1994.

Curtis, William J. R. *Modern Architecture Since 1900*. Phaidon Press, London 1982.

Czech Functionalism 1918–1938. Foreword by Gustav Peichl. Architectural Association, London 1987.

Davies, Colin. *High-Tech Architecture*. Thames & Hudson, London 1988.

Davies, Colin. *Michael Hopkins: The Work of Michael Hopkins and Partners*. Phaidon, London 1993.

Davis, Mike. *City of Quartz: Excavating the Future in Los Angeles*. Verso, London 1990.

De Long, David. *Bruce Goff: Towards Absolute Architecture*. Architectural History Foundation and MIT Press, Cambridge, MA 1988.

Dunham, Judith. *Details of Frank Lloyd Wright: The California Work 1919–1974*. Thames & Hudson, London 1994.

Education of the Architect, The. Edited by Martha Pollak. MIT Press, Cambridge, MA 1997.

Egelius, Mats. *Ralph Erskine, Architect*. Byggforlaget in conjunction with the Swedish Museum of Architecture, Stockholm 1991.

Encyclopedia of 20th Century Architecture. Edited by Vittorio Lampugnani. Thames & Hudson, London 1983 (first published by Droernersche Verlagsanstalt, Munich 1963).

Energy in Architecture: The European Passive Solar Handbook. Edited by J. R. Goulding, J. Owen Lewis and Theo C. Steemers. Batsford, London 1992.

Esher, Lionel. *A Broken Wave: The Rebuilding of England 1940–1980*. Allen Lane, London 1981.

Ferriss, Hugh. *Power in Buildings: An Artist's View of Contemporary Architecture*. Columbia University Press, New York 1953.

Filter of Reason, The. The Work of Paul Nelson. Edited by Terence Riley and Joseph Abram. Rizzoli International, London 1990.

Fletcher, Sir Banister. *A History of Architecture on the Comparative Method*, XVII edition. Edited by J. C. Palmes. RIBA, London 1976.

Foster, Norman. *Selected and Current works of Foster and Partners*. Images, Mulgrave, Australia 1997.

Frampton, Kenneth. *Modern Architecture: A Critical History*. Thames & Hudson, London 1980.

Fry, E. Maxwell. *Fine Building*. Faber & Faber, London 1944.

Gill, Brendan. *Many Masks: a Life of Frank Lloyd Wright*. Heinemann, London 1987.

Glendinning, Miles and Stefan Muthesius. *Tower Block: Modern Public Housing in England, Scotland, Wales and Northern Ireland*. Yale University Press, New Haven, CT 1994.

Gooding, Mel. *William Alsop: Buildings and Projects*. Phaidon, London 1992.

Gropius, Walter. *The Scope of Total Architecture*. George Allen & Unwin, London 1956.

Harper, Roger H. *Victorian Architectural Competitions 1843–1900*. Mansell, London 1983.

Herbert, Gilbert. *The Dream of the Factory-made House*. MIT Press, Cambridge, MA 1985.

Hitchcock, Henry Russell and Philip Johnson. *The International Style*: *Architecture Since 1922*. Museum of Modern Art, New York 1932.

Hix, John. *The Glasshouse*. Phaidon, London 1996.

Hochman, Elaine S. *Mies van der Rohe and the Third Reich*. Weidenfeld & Nicolson, London 1989.

Holston, James. *The Modernist City*. Chicago University Press, Chicago 1990.

Housing the Airship. Edited by Christopher Dean. The Architectural Association, London 1989.

Huxtable, Ada Louise. *The Tall Building Artistically Considered*. Pantheon, New York 1984/Trefoil, London 1986.

Jackson, Anthony. *The Politics of Architecture: A History of Modern Architecture in Britain*. Architectural Press, London 1970.

James Stirling, Buildings and Projects. Edited by Peter Arnell and Ted Bickford. Architectural Press, London 1984.

Jencks, Charles. *Architecture 2000*. Studio Vista, London 1971.

Jencks, Charles. *Modern Movements in Architecture*. Anchor Press, New York 1973.

Jencks, Charles. *The Language of Postmodern Architecture*. Academy Editions, London 1976.

Jencks, Charles. *The Prince, the Architects, and New Wave Monarchy*. Academy Editions, London 1988.

Jencks, Charles. *Heteropolis: Los Angeles, the Riots and the Strange Beauty of Hetero-Architecture*. Academy Group, London 1993.

Jencks, Charles. *The Architecture of the Jumping Universe*. Academy Editions, London 1995.

Kopp, Anatole. *Constructivist Architecture in the USSR*. Academy Editions, London 1985.

Kostof, Spiro. *The City Assembled: The Elements of Urban Form Through History*. Thames & Hudson, London 1993.

Krier, Leon. *Albert Speer, Architecture 1932–1942*. Academy des Arts, Brussels 1985.

Krier, Leon. *Architecture and Urban Design*. Academy Editions, London 1993.

Krier, Rob. *Architecture and Urban Design*. Academy Editions/ Ernst & Sohn, London 1994.

Kronenburg, Robert. *Houses in Motion: The Genesis, History and Development of the Portable Building*. Academy Editions, London 1995.

Kubler, George. *The Shape of Time*. Yale University Press, New Haven, CT 1962.

Kurokawa, Kisho. *New Wave Japanese Architecture*. Academy Editions/Ernst & Sohn, London 1993.

Leon Krier: Architecture and Urban Design. Edited by Richard Economakis. Academy Editions, London 1993.

Lloyd Wright, Frank. *The Future of Architecture*. Horizon, New York 1953.

Longstreth, Richard. *City Centre to Regional Mall: Architecture, the Automobile and Retailing in Los Angeles 1920–1950*. MIT Press, Cambridge, MA 1997.

Loos, Adolf. *Spoken into the Void: Collected Essays*. Adolf Opel, Vienna 1981 (first published by Georges Cres, Paris 1921).

Lowenthal, David and Marcus Binney. *Our Past Before Us*. Temple, London 1981.

Lustenberger, Kurt. *Adolf Loos*. Artemis, London 1994.

Mallory, Keith and Arvid Ottar. *The Architecture of Aggression*. Architectural Press, London 1973.

Marks, Robert and Richard Buckminster Fuller. *The Dymaxion World of Buckminster Fuller*. University of Southern Illinois, Carbondale, IL 1960.

Markus, Thomas A. *Buildings and Power: Freedom and Control in the Origin of Modern Building Types*. Routledge, London 1993.

Metcalf, Thomas. *An Imperial Vision*. Faber & Faber, London 1989.

Miller Lane, Barbara. *Architecture and Politics in Germany 1918–1945*. Harvard University Press, Cambridge, MA 1968.

Mitchell, Peter. *Memento Mori: The Flats at Quarry Hill, Leeds*. Smith Settle, Otley 1990.

Moderne Architektur in Deutschland: Reform und Tradition. Deutsches Architektur-Museum, Frankfurt-am-Main 1992 (Exhibition Catalogue).

Muthesius, Hermann. *The English House*, 3 volumes. Wasmuth, Berlin 1904–1905.

Neutra, Richard. *Survival Through Design*. Oxford University Press, Oxford 1954.

New Classicism: Omnibus Volume. Edited by Andreas Papadakis and Harriet Watson. Foreword by Leon Krier. Academy Editions, London 1990.

Norman Foster. *Foster Associates. Buildings and Projects 1964–1989*, 4 volumes. Edited by Ian Lambot. Watermark, London.

OMA, Rem Koolhaas and Bruce Mau. *S,M,L,XL*. Uitgeverij 010, Rotterdam 1997.

Our Past Before Us: Why do We Save It? Edited by David Lowenthal and Marcus Binney. Temple Smith, London 1981.

Papanek, Victor. *Design for the Real World*, 2nd edition, completely revised. Academy Chicago Publishers, Chicago 1986.

Papanek, Victor. *Design for Human Scale*. Van Nostrand Reinhold, New York 1986.

Pawley, Martin. *Building for Tomorrow: Putting Waste to Work*. Sierra Club, San Francisco 1982.

Pawley, Martin. *Buckminster Fuller*. Trefoil, London 1990.

Pawley, Martin. *Theory and Design in the Second Machine Age*. Blackwell, Oxford 1991.

Pawley, Martin. *Future Systems: The Story of Tomorrow*. Phaidon, London 1993.

Pearce, David. *Conservation Today*. Routledge, London 1989.

Pearson, Paul David. *Alvar Aalto and the International Style*. Mitchell, London 1989 (first published by Batsford, London 1978).

Pevsner, Nikolaus. *Pioneers of Modern Design: From William Morris to Walter Gropius*. Pelican, London 1938.

Porter, Tom. *How Architects Visualize*. Van Nostrand Reinhold, New York 1979.

Powell, C. G. *An Economic History of the British Building Industry 1815–1979*. Architectural Press, London 1980.

Prak, Niels. *Architects: the Noted and the Ignored*. Wiley, New York 1984.

Rand, Ayn. *The Fountainhead*. Norton, Boston, MA 1936.

Reading, Malcolm and Peter Coe. *Lubetkin and Tecton: An Architectural Study*. Triangle Architectural Publishing, London 1993.

Renzo Piano Logbook, The. Preface by Kenneth Frampton. Thames & Hudson, London 1997.

Rice, Peter. *An Engineer Imagines*. Artemis, London 1994.

Richard Rogers + Architects. Architectural Monographs Series edited by Frank Russell. Academy Editions, London 1986.

Richards, James. *Modern Architecture*. Penguin, London 1950.

Rogers, Richard. *Cities for a Small Planet*. Edited by Philip Gumuchdjian. Faber & Faber, London 1997.

Ryn, Sim Van der and Peter Calthorpe. *Sustainable Communities: A New Design Synthesis for Cities, Suburbs and Towns*. Sierra Club, San Francisco 1986.

Sabbagh, Karl. *Skyscraper: The Making of a Building*. Macmillan, New York 1989.

Saint, Andrew. *The Image of the Architect*. Yale University Press, New Haven, CT 1983.

Saint, Andrew. *Towards a Social Architecture: The Role of School Building in Post-war England*. Yale University Press, New Haven, CT 1987.

Schon, Donald. *The Reflective Practitioner*. Temple Smith, London 1983.

Scruton, Roger. *The Classical Vernacular: Architectural Principles in an Age of Nihilism*. Carcanet Press, London 1994.

Schultze, Franz. *Mies van der Rohe: A Critical Biography*. University of Chicago Press, Chicago 1986.

Sieden, Lloyd Steven. *Buckminster Fuller's Universe: An Appreciation*. Plenum Press, New York 1989.

Senger, Axel von. *Die Brackenfels Moskaus (Moscow's Torch)*. Switzerland 1930 (publisher unknown).

Shepheard, Paul. *What is Architecture? An Essay on Landscapes, Buildings and Machines*. MIT Press, Cambridge, MA 1994.

Smithson, Alison and Peter Smithson. *Without Rhetoric: An Architectural Aesthetic*. MIT Press, Cambridge, Mass. 1973.

Sobel, Robert. *Trammell Crow, Master Builder: The Story of America's Largest Real Estate Empire*. Wiley, New York 1991.

Sodre, Nelson W. *Oscar Niemeyer*. Editora Revan, Rio de Janeiro 1978.

Spade, Rupert. *Masters of Modern Architecture: Oscar Niemeyer*. Thames & Hudson, London 1971.

Speer, Albert. *Inside the Third Reich*. Weidenfeld & Nicolson, London 1971.

Spence, Basil. *Phoenix at Coventry*. Geoffrey Bles, London 1962.

Storrer, William Allin. *The Frank Lloyd Wright Companion*. University of Chicago Press, Chicago 1993.

Structure, Space and Skin: The Work of Nicholas Grimshaw & Partners. Edited by Rowan Moore. Phaidon, London 1993.

Sudjic, Deyan. *The 100 Mile City*. Andre Deutsch, London 1992.

Sudjic, Deyan. *The Architecture of Richard Rogers*. 4th Estate, London 1994.

Tegethoff, Wolf. *Mies van der Rohe: The Villas and Country Houses*. MIT Press, Cambridge, MA 1986.

Vale, Brenda and Robert Vale. *Green Architecture: Design for a Sustainable Future*. Thames & Hudson, London 1991.

Venturi, Robert. *Complexity and Contradiction in Architecture*. Museum of Modern Art, New York 1966.

Vision of Europe: Architecture and Urbanism for the European City. Edited by Gabriele Tagliaventi and Liam O'Connor. Foreword by HRH Prince of Wales. Alinea Editrice, Florence 1992.

Wachsmann. Konrad. *The Turning Point of Building: Structure and Design*. Reinhold, New York 1961.

Wales, HRH the Prince of. *A Vision of Britain*. Doubleday, London 1989.

Wales, HRH the Prince of and Charles Clover. *Highgrove: Portrait of an Estate*. Chapmans, London 1992.

Watkin, David. *A History of Western Architecture*. Century Hutchinson, London 1986.

Whittick, Arnold. *European Architecture in the Twentieth Century*, 2 Volumes. Crosby Lockwood, London 1950/1953.

Wilkinson, Chris. *Supersheds: The Architecture of Long-span, Large-volume Buildings*. Butterworth Architecture, Oxford 1991.

Wise, Michael Z. *Capital Dilemma: Germany's Search for a New Architecture of Democracy*. Princeton Architectural Press, Princeton, NJ 1998.

Wolfe, Tom. *From Bauhaus to our House*. Farrar Straus, Giroux, New York 1981.

Yorke, Frederick. *The Modern House*. Architectural Press, London 1934.

Yorke, Frederick. *A Key to Modern Architecture*. Blackie, London 1939.

Zuk, William and Roger Clark. *Kinetic Architecture*. Van Nostrand Reinhold, New York 1970.

Index